Kingdom Power

By Prayer And Fasting

The key to releasing the power of God!

(Second Edition)

Jerry Scheidbach

Executive Editor, *The Intercessor* magazine

Hearing Heart Publications

A division of

Distinctively Baptist

P u b l i c a t i o n s

Copyright © 2012 by Jerry Scheidbach

Kingdom Power By Prayer And Fasting
(Second Edition)
Jerry Scheidbach

Printed in the United States of America

ISBN: 9780982211014 (previously published 5.5x8.5, paper, hard back, and ebook, by Xulon Press – ISBN: 9781619965522)

All Bible quotations are taken from the Authorized King James Version.

Proofreading: Barbara Melander, Becky Scheidbach

Cover Design: Nakia Jones

The author, Jerry Scheidbach, pastors the Lighthouse Baptist Church in Santa Maria, California. He is the executive editor for *The Intercessor* magazine, and hosts *The Brain Massage* radio show. To contact Pastor Scheidbach write to Lighthouse Baptist Church, PO Box 2803, Santa Maria, CA 93457, or call (805) 347-9887. To contact him by email visit our websites at www.santamarialighthouse.org or www.thebrainmassageshow.com and click on the Contact Us button.

Foreword

I recommend you read *Kingdom Power By Prayer And Fasting* with a prayer on your heart, a Bible in your hand, and with your thoughts brought into captivity to the obedience of Christ. If you do, you will learn how to tap into the dynamic power of God's Kingdom.

In studying the chapters of this book, you will learn what it means to pray and fast, and why it is vital that you should do it. In finishing the book, you will find that you are equipped to fight the Devil. In studying these pages, you will learn that the only way to win victory over some devils is through "prayer and fasting" (Matthew 17:21).

I'm glad you purchased this book. I know that when you have read it, you will be a stronger Christian, and you will be challenged to practice prayer and fasting in your life. We desperately need people like you who will be recruited to join us in God's great war against His enemy and ours. For the future of the Lord's churches and this great nation, I exhort you to read and heed the message of this book.

Dr. Benny L. Beckum
Founder/President
Intercessor Ministries, Inc.

– Table Of Contents –

Introduction

Does it seem to you that Satan is getting the upper hand in your nation, your church, your home, and even in your personal life?

How can this be? Satan has been defeated, right? (John 12:31; 16:11) The Spirit that is in us is greater than the spirit that is in this world, right? Doesn't the Bible say, "Greater is He that is in you than he that is in the world"? (I John 4:4) And haven't we been told that if we "resist the devil" he will "flee" from us? (James 4:7) So why does it seem that the Spirit of Jesus Christ is losing influence in this world while the spirit of antichrist is gaining greater control?

Jesus warned us that during His absence we would face powerful devils of the kind that can only be overcome by prayer and fasting (Matthew 17:21). Such devils have established strongholds in our personal lives, in our homes, in our churches and in this nation. It seems the enemy is massing an army of evil that is about to overwhelm us like a flood. The only way we are going to survive is to overcome these devils, and the only way we will succeed at that is to do what Jesus told us was the only way to address such devils as these — *by prayer and fasting*.

In the chapters that follow, you will learn how to use

the most powerful spiritual weapon the Christian has in his or her arsenal—the weapon of prayer with fasting.

Prayer and fasting is truly the lost key to Kingdom power in this world. Read this book to understand what fasting is, what it does, why it works, and how to do it. Then, do it! For the sake of your country, and your church, for the sake of your children and theirs, for your own sake, but more importantly, for Jesus' sake—fast and pray!

Was Jesus embarrassed? Some disciples of John had challenged Him with an accusation against His disciples: "Why do we and the Pharisees fast oft, but thy disciples fast not?" (Matthew 9:14). Jesus explained that so long as He, the bridegroom, was present with them, they could not fast, because they could not mourn (Matthew 9:15; Mark 2:19). "But," He said, "the days will come, when the bridegroom shall be taken away from them, and then shall they fast in those days" (Mark 2:20). He thought we would fast.

Perhaps the Lord was not embarrassed for His disciples on that day, since, as He explained, they could not fast while He was with them. However, Jesus has been taken away from us into Heaven (Acts 1:9). We can be sure that the accuser of the brethren misses no opportunity to chide our Lord daily with the accusation that so few of His disciples bother to fast for Him today.

Many fast for health reasons. Some fast to gratify the perverse hunger of spiritual pride. Others fast to win an argument, and even to seek vengeance upon their enemies. Few are moved to fast by a deep yearning for His return, or for a fresh manifestation of His Kingdom power to release those who are oppressed by His enemy, and ours (Isaiah 58:3-7).

Jesus assumed His disciples would fast because they would mourn His absence. But do not make the mistake of thinking He was talking about a vain, sentimental desire to see Him. He knew what we would face while He was away, and He knew that fasting would be necessary because He would not be here to take care of those devils that can only be handled by prayer and fasting.

Why is it important for us to fast and pray until He returns?

A pitiful scene it must have been! The father of a demon-possessed son came to the disciples for help. His son had been tormented by a devil since he was a child, and the family was desperate. No doubt they heard about the amazing power the disciples of Jesus had demonstrated over devils, and when this father heard they were nearby, he took his son to them for help. They tried to help but could not. Pitiful indeed! Here was a child tormented by a powerful devil, a father desperate to find help for his son, and the disciples of Jesus Christ, famous for their power over devils (Matthew 10:1), powerless to help.

Jesus was away! He had taken Peter, James, and John into a mountain where He was transfigured before them into His Kingdom glory (Matthew 17:1-13). Moses and

Elijah visited them there, and the Father spoke aloud—it was a touch of Heaven on earth. The other nine disciples were left below to face this devil that would not bow to their power. Perplexed, and vexed, in part because they truly desired to help this tormented child and relieve the burden of this desperate father, and in part, because they were bewildered, and chagrined. If only Jesus were there, or at least one of the three chief apostles, surely they could drive out this devil.

Smug scribes had gathered around the confused disciples and were asking questions. The powerlessness of these followers of Jesus was becoming an embarrassment (Mark 9:16). Since the day that Jesus had given them power over devils, they had never come up against one they could not command. Why were they powerless against this one? If only Jesus were there! He could explain why they were unable to cast out this particular devil. But He was away and they were alone.

Happily, He had not yet gone into Heaven. He returned to them from the mountain. When he arrived, the case of the devil–possessed child was brought before Him. Jesus' rebuke must have stung the disciples! "O faithless and perverse generation, how long shall I be with you? How long shall I suffer you? Bring him hither to me" (Matthew 17:17).

Jesus needed His disciples to learn some vital lessons about dealing with devils before He departed "into a far country for a long time" (Luke 20:9).

After Jesus commanded the devil to depart from the child and never return (Mark 9:25), the "spirit cried, and rent him sore, and came out of him" (Mark 9:26). The disciples waited until they were alone with the Chief Shepherd and then sheepishly asked Him, "Why could not we cast him out?" (Mark 9:28) Jesus' explanation provides the title, and declares the purpose of this book: "This kind can come forth by nothing, but by prayer and fasting" (Mark 9:29).

Kingdom Power By Prayer and Fasting provides instruction and insight into the relationship between prayer and fasting and Kingdom power that will help you become a more effective disciple of Jesus Christ.

Jesus is away in heavenly Zion. He is not here with us to rebuke the devils that torment our children and get in the way of Kingdom work. But He has given us His Spirit, and commissioned Him to reprove the world, commanding all men to repent and believe on the Lord Jesus Christ. Jesus prophesied that His Spirit would flow through our belly into the world (John 7:38-39).

Be aware that there is another spirit at work in the world: the prince of the power of the air, the "spirit that now worketh in the children of disobedience" (Ephesians 2:2). Lucifer, also called Satan or the Devil, is this prince. And, with his horde of demons, he seduces men by doctrines of devils to advance the cause of the spirit of antichrist in the world (I Timothy 4:1-4). His cause is to overthrow the rule of Christ in the earth and set up his kingdom of darkness in its place.

Jesus' Spirit flows through our belly (John 7:38-39). Through us, the Spirit of Christ restrains the spirit of antichrist (I John 4:3; see II Thessalonians 2:7).

Apparently, sometimes the belly becomes clogged with what the world offers and must be opened by *prayer and fasting* to release the *flow*.

The conflict between the Spirit of Jesus Christ and the spirit of antichrist is what we call *spiritual warfare*. This book is a compilation of articles written by the author for *The Intercessor* magazine on the subject of prayer and fasting. It is intended to serve as a primer that will prepare the reader for his sequel, providing a comprehensive study of spiritual warfare, titled, *God's War: Understanding Spiritual Warfare.* Together, these books will help believers become effective in fulfilling their role as soldiers in God's war (II Timothy 2:3-4).

The urgency of the message cannot be overstated. The current generation of believers is perverse, faithless, and has given over much *place* to the Devil (Ephesians 4:27). Satan has strengthened his seat in the world by appointing powerful devils to hold places of authority that we've given him. Devils of the kind mentioned in the story above can only be driven back *by prayer and fasting*. So what is keeping you from becoming a mighty warrior who can accomplish great and miraculous things for God's Kingdom? Let's find out!

Throughout this book, you will be encouraged to reflect on the status of your own faith. You will be confronted with truths that will answer many questions you have about why the Devil seems to get the upper hand in your life, and in the lives of your family and friends. You will receive insights that will help you take back ground you've lost to the enemy, and break the oppression of Satan over your own life, and the lives of your family, friends, and neighbors. Personal challenges will be offered at the end of each chapter for you to consider that will make you wiser, stronger, and more prepared to engage in spiritual warfare as an effective soldier of the Lord Jesus Christ. Begin the adventure of charging the gates of Hell *by prayer and fasting.*

Chapter One

What Is It, What Does It Do, And Why Should We Do It?

"Prayer is reaching out after the unseen; fasting is letting go of all that is seen and temporal. Fasting helps express, deepen, confirm the resolution that we are ready to sacrifice anything, even ourselves to attain what we seek for the kingdom of God."

— Andrew Murray

Popular Christianity wants to clap its hands, and shout, and laugh; it does not want to weep or mourn. And it certainly is not inclined to deprive the flesh of its pleasures, much less its necessary food. But the Early Church practiced fasting (Acts 13:2, 3; 14:23). Paul gave instruction to couples that included a reference to fasting that shows it was common among believers in the early churches (I Corinthians 7:5). We should not be surprised, for Jesus had given specific instructions about fasting to His disciples (Matthew 6:15-18). He even told them why it would be necessary.

His disciples once attempted to cast out a demon and could not (Matthew 17:14-23). The possessed young man was brought to Jesus, Who rebuked the devil and it departed. The disciples asked why they could not cast it out and Jesus explained it was because of their unbelief.

But then He added, "Howbeit this kind goeth not out but by prayer and fasting" (Matthew 17:21).

When they came to Jesus for help, He rebuked them, "O faithless and perverse generation, how long shall I be with you?" (Matthew 17:17). He explained that the spiritual power needed to deal with this kind of demon required fasting and prayer. While He was with them, He was there to take care of it. But He knew that He would be leaving, and that His disciples would need fasting and prayer to have the power necessary to handle some levels of Satanic oppression and opposition. The Early Church understood this. Popular Christianity had better let its laughter be turned to mourning (James 4:9). It had better learn to fast and pray. For the demons of Hell are pursuing our children, and among them are devils that, "goeth not out but by prayer and fasting."

What is Fasting?

Fasting is abstinence from nourishment for a spiritual purpose. Two questions arise. First, does fasting require abstinence from both food and water? And second, what is the spiritual purpose of fasting?

The Scripture expressly notes that Moses abstained from both food and water during his forty-days fast (Exodus 34:28). Although the Scripture is not so explicit in the account of Elijah's forty-days fast, the language of the text inclines me to conclude he abstained from both food and water (I Kings 19:8). Some think Jesus abstained from food, but did receive water during His forty-days fast. This conclusion is based on Luke 4:2, "And in those days he did eat nothing …" The assumption is that because the Spirit did specify that Moses abstained from both, but did not make this clear regarding Jesus' fast, that, therefore, Jesus had water during His forty-days fast. But the most that can be said is that Luke 4:2 leaves the question open. I believe Jesus abstained from both food and water. And I think the essential idea of fasting involves abstaining from both. However, this is not to say fasting food-only is not a legitimate fast. Because the effectiveness of fasting is not so much in this formal technicality as it is in achieving the effect and obtaining the purpose of fasting.

What is the purpose of fasting?

"The purpose of fasting is to loosen to some degree the ties which bind us to the world of material things…that we may concentrate all our spiritual powers upon the unseen and eternal things." O. Hallesby

Jesus was glorified in the presence of His special entourage, Peter, James, and John, on a mount we have come to call the Mount of Transfiguration (Matthew 17:1). Moses and Elijah appeared there with Jesus. Isn't it interesting that these three are distinguished as having profound spiritual power, and each fasted forty days?

That is certainly an elite club. But what is more interesting to the purpose of this article is the fact that when Jesus and His special entourage returned from the mountain, Jesus revealed something about fasting that speaks very directly to its purpose.

The transfiguration was a manifestation of the Kingdom of God on earth. While Jesus, Peter, James and John were away, the other disciples encountered a devil they could not command. When Jesus returned to them, He made it clear the only way to access the level of Kingdom power needed in this case was by prayer and fasting. Clearly, Matthew 17 is intended to present a message to us about the need for and the purpose of fasting.

First, we see a representation of the Kingdom of God on earth, and the three persons assembled there representing this Kingdom authority are each noteworthy as having fasted forty days. Then, Jesus comes down from the mountain, and informs the disciples that His time with them is limited, and therefore, to have the power of the Kingdom necessary to deal with this special kind of demon power, they would need to fast and pray. The message of Matthew 17 is clear – fasting and prayer, together, are essential to have the Kingdom power we need to do the work that needs to be done during Jesus' absence. The essential purpose of fasting and prayer is to secure the spiritual power needed to accomplish the work that could otherwise only be done by Jesus. We must not miss the obvious point that our Lord Jesus, and Moses and Elijah are each noted as having fasted forty days, with the fact that these three demonstrated spiritual power beyond any other personalities in the Bible. The connection between fasting and prayer and spiritual power cannot be missed, must not be missed. The devils of Hell are after our ministries, and among them are devils that "goeth not out but by prayer and fasting."

What does fasting do?

Jesus had a wonderful vision, and I am afraid we have disappointed Him. He prophesied that from our belly would flow rivers of living water (John 7:38-39). The Spirit, by John, explained that He was talking about the coming of the Holy Spirit, and the fact that He would be working through our lives; that is, flowing from our belly into this world (John 7:38-39). Fasting opens the door of the belly to allow the Spirit to flow. Let me explain.

Our *heart* is the spiritual center of our lives. It is closely associated with our spiritual affections, and our thoughts (Hebrews 4:12). It is the dwelling place of the Spirit of God (Galatians 4:6). By contrast, the *belly* represents the physical center of our lives, or the flesh; it represents the center of our physical appetites, our carnal desires. The *heart* is our point of closest contact with the spiritual world, and the *belly* is our point of closest contact with the physical world.

When we get saved, the Spirit takes up residence in our heart. But He does not flow through us into the world through our heart. He flows through our lives into the world through our belly. In other words, our physical appetites, our carnal desires, must be surrendered to His control in order for the Spirit to flow through our lives into the world around us.

There are those whose god is their belly (Philippians 3:19). They "mind earthly things." The belly is associated with our appetites, or that which we covet. We make an idol of what we covet when we put what we covet before God. This is New Testament idolatry, for covetousness is the sin of idolatry (Colossians 3:5). When we surrender to coveting, our thoughts become fixated on earthly things, so we "mind earthly things." Remember, Paul, by the Spirit, said that those who are spiritual would mind "the things of the Spirit." He warned, "to be carnally minded is death" (Romans 8:5-6). He explained that to walk in the Spirit, we must mind "the things of the Spirit." You can see that the key is to destroy the idols of covetousness in our lives.

Our soul is intimately connected to our belly (Psalm 31:9; 44:25; Proverbs 13:25; Leviticus 7:20). This explains what the Spirit revealed through David when he wrote, "I humbled my soul with fasting" (Psalm 35:13). By depriving the belly of its necessary food, the flesh is weakened, and this, coupled with intense, fervent prayer, effects a corresponding humbling of the soul. When our soul becomes lifted up in pride (Psalm

24:4), we must humble ourselves under the mighty hand of God (I Peter 5:6). Starving the belly humbles the soul.

We must lift up our soul to the Lord (Psalm 25:1; 86:4; 143:8). But when we commit the wicked sin of idolatry through coveting, we are lifting up our soul to vanity. This is an arrogant and prideful thing to do. God resists the proud, but He gives grace to the lowly (I Peter 5:5). We must heed the Spirit's warning and avoid the lusts of the flesh that "war against the soul" (I Peter 2:11). The belly is the center of our physical appetites; it's the place where our soul intersects with the world around us. We need to turn our soul from the idols of covetousness to the Lord of Glory. For when we serve the idols of covetousness, the thoughts of our heart are fixated on fleshly lusts (Romans 8:5-6), and our affections are perverted into lustful desires, and this grieves the Spirit (Ephesians 4:30) so that He will not fill His temple, our body (I Corinthians 6:19), and flow through our belly into the world (John 7:38-39).

Fasting with prayer serves to break the idols of covetousness by weakening the strength of fleshly appetites over us and humbling the soul.

Something to think about:

1. Jesus expected us to fast after He was taken into Heaven (Mark 2:20). Have you ever completed a time of fasting with prayers? If not, why not?

2. Do you sometimes feel like your spiritual senses are dull, and your spirit sluggish with respect to the things of God? According to what you have learned so far, how can prayer with fasting help?

3. What did you learn about the relationship between the soul and the belly? What happens to our soul when we periodically deprive the belly of food?

4. The Spirit, by Peter and James, said God resists the proud, but gives grace to the lowly (James 4:6; I Peter 5:5). How important is God's grace to our lives? With this in mind, what is the relationship between prayer and fasting and receiving the grace of God?

Chapter Two

Sincere Fasting! (Why does God sometimes reject our fasts?)

"Many people not only lose the benefit, but are even the worse for their mortifications [such as fasting] … because they mistake the whole nature and worth of them: they practice them for their own sakes, as things good in themselves, they think them to be real parts of holiness, and so rest in them and look no further, but grow full of a self-esteem and self-admiration for their own progress in them. This makes them self-sufficient, morose, severe judges of all those that fall short of their mortifications. And thus their self-denials do only that for them which indulgences do for other people: they withstand and hinder the operation of God upon their souls, and instead of being really self-denials, they strengthen and keep up the kingdom of self."

– William Law

The dumbing down of discipleship has cost us more than we know. We are overdue for revival in America — a revival so necessary that if we do not have it, this nation will perish from the earth. More than 65 million children daily are exposed to the godless philosophy of paganism that permeates our post-modern culture and humanistic public schools, while only about 12 million children attend Sunday school, one hour a week, and most of them are learning very little Bible. And those who are learning some Bible are not challenged to rise to the call of Jesus for disciples who strive to "be perfect" (Deuteronomy 18:13; II Corinthians 13:11; Philippians 3:15; II Timothy 3:17), and to "walk worthy of the Lord unto all pleasing," (Colossians 1:10; see I Thessalonians 2:12), or to *deny self* and take up their cross to follow Him (Matthew 16:24; Luke 9:23; see Galatians 2:20).

Perhaps some reading this balk at the call to "be perfect." Isn't it interesting how the world has morphed the sense of certain words so that when we speak *according to this word* and say, "be perfect," those who speak according to this world think we are talking about sinless perfection? Pay attention — the seducing spirits are always saying, "You can't be perfect" and "no one is worthy." And in our spiritually dull condition, we have failed to recognize the hiss of the serpent in that ungodly language — even repeating it ourselves — dumbing down discipleship.

We complain about a public school system that gives diplomas to students who can't read and yet we give the name *disciple* to those whose carnal lifestyles besmirch the name of Jesus and encourage the mock of devils. What does this have to do with fasting? Discipleship has gotten cheaper with every passing generation. Today, most actually believe it to be as free as salvation. But Jesus told us to count the cost. To rise up against the onslaught of the activity of devils attacking

21

America today, we are going to need disciples of Jesus Christ who recognize that the cost of discipleship includes fasting with prayers.

Mourning moves us to fasting and prayer. Jesus said His disciples could not "mourn" while the Bridegroom was with them, and therefore they could not fast (Matthew 9:15). The Bridegroom has ascended into Heaven (Acts 1:5-11). Jesus expected us to fast in these days, mourning His absence. And so the Spirit exhorts us to "be afflicted, and mourn, and weep: let your laughter be turned to mourning, and your joy to heaviness" (James 4:9). If we were appropriately mindful of our condition, and the condition of this world, we would mourn; this mourning would move us to chasten our soul with fasting until we joined the fellowship of the Spirit (Philippians 2:1), the communion of the Holy Ghost (II Corinthians 13:14), Who makes intercession for us "with groanings which cannot be uttered" (Romans 8:26).

Fasting is about mourning the absence of our Lord and joining in the communion of the Holy Ghost, Who intercedes on our behalf with unutterable groaning (Romans 8:26). Therefore, the first step in fasting is to consciously commit yourself to *let* (allow) your laughter to be *turned to mourning.* The Spirit said, "let," and this tells us His influence works on us to draw us in that direction.

But we do always resist the Holy Ghost, and so we add grief to His groaning (Ephesians 4:30-31).

As I said before, the Church today only wants a *Christianity* that laughs, and sings, so it knows nothing of true joy because it refuses to follow Him, to *let* its laughter be turned to mourning. The *joy* such churches enjoy is superficial and only lasts so long as the music is playing, loudly, and the service encourages a romantic kind of love for God instead of that holy, reverent, humbling love of Christ that prayed, "not my will, but Thine be done."

O, my dearly beloved, consider. Our spiritual senses are dulled by our drunkenness on pleasure and ease. Hear the Spirit groan, "Be sober, be vigilant; because your adversary the devil ... (seeks) whom he may devour" (I Peter 5:8). The pleasure drunkards need to dry out, to let their laughter be turned to mourning; and this beckons us to fast and pray.

Sincere fasting is the subject of Isaiah 58:5, "Is it such a fast that I have chosen? a day for a man to afflict his soul? is it to bow down his head as a bulrush, and to spread sackcloth and ashes under him? wilt thou call this a fast, and an acceptable day to the LORD?"

At first glance, it would appear the Lord is complaining against these particular forms that accompany fasting: bowing of the head, and the use of sackcloth and ashes, for example. You must check the context of the passage to know that God is not rejecting the *forms* that are associated with fasting. Indeed, He has shown favor to believers who have openly displayed their self-affliction of the soul, bowing their head as a bulrush, and using sackcloth and ashes as public tokens of mourning. Consider the following testimony from Scripture that these forms are acceptable to the Lord:

Leviticus 16:29, "And this shall be a statute for ever unto you: that in the seventh month, on the tenth day of the month, ye shall afflict your souls …."

Psalm 95:6, "O come, let us worship and bow down …."

Genesis 24:26, "And the man bowed down his head, and worshipped the LORD."

Esther 4:1, "When Mordecai perceived all that was done, Mordecai rent his clothes, and put on sackcloth with ashes …."

Jeremiah 6:26, "O daughter of my people, gird thee with sackcloth, and wallow thyself in ashes: make thee mourning …."

Daniel 9:3, "And I set my face unto the Lord God, to seek by prayer and supplications, with fasting, and sackcloth, and ashes."

The context of Isaiah 58 makes it clear it is the use of these forms insincerely, to be seen of men, that God rejects. The pride that motivates such insincere flaunting of the *form of godliness* is what God despises. Indeed, such prideful display produces the exact opposite result that is sought, for "God resisteth the proud" (James 4:6). Grace is extended to the humble.

Who is so foolish as to imagine that the pride that makes these forms repugnant to our flesh is any less repugnant to God?

Go ahead and put on sackcloth and see how the flesh likes it.

How often do we disdain to move forward in a service to kneel and pray before others because of our pride?

Do we disdain the form because it humbles our flesh?

Whether we resist public display of our mourning because of pride, or put our mourning on public display in service to our pride, it is pride nevertheless.

Fasting is serious business. It must be done sincerely. Modern Christianity has followed seducing spirits in their disdain for ancient forms of worship. But, that these forms do have influence with God, when used sincerely, is evident all over the Scriptures (see those references above). Even wicked Ahab was heard of God when he humbled himself publicly in this manner (I Kings 21:25-29).

I'm not suggesting that unless you don sackcloth and ashes you are not sincere about your fast. Indeed, the point of Isaiah 58 is that any influence these forms might have with God is cancelled unless they are done sincerely. I am saying that the modern churches' disdain for forms or outward displays of humility has corroded the piety of the believers as much as hypocrisy has corroded the piety of those who displayed those forms insincerely.

Something to think about:

1. Contrast the attitude evident in most worship today with the exhortation to "let your laughter be turned to mourning..." What relationship does fasting have with mourning? How might fasting change you, your home, and your church?

2. What dulls our spiritual senses? What is the relationship between fasting and sharpening our spiritual senses?

3. Name some of the forms used to demonstrate humility before God that are mentioned in this chapter. Have you ever wrapped yourself in sackcloth to pray? Have you ever sprinkled dust, or ashes, upon your head? Why not? Think it through! Is it because you would feel silly? Perhaps it is because you don't understand the significance of these forms. Maybe you should do a study of how these forms were used and what they mean.

Chapter Three

Serious Fasting!

"As men and women are beginning to consider the days and times through which we are passing with a new seriousness, and as many are beginning to look for revival and reawakening, the question of fasting has become more and more important."

– D. Martyn Lloyd-Jones

You have heard the statistic and I'm sure it has baffled you; 76% of Americans identify themselves as *born again*. But we continue to countenance the murder of over one million babies a year; judges who want to post the Ten Commandments are fired, while liberal jurists debate whether "In God We Trust" is legal for legal tender; and many want to make it a crime to call sodomy sin. However, when you learn that only 41% of Americans believe the Bible is totally accurate in all that it teaches, that divorce is as common among Christians as it is in the world, and that more born-again Christians believe in channeling, astrology and reincarnation than non born-again Christians, it all begins to make sense. Many who claim to be born again are not (Matthew 7:22-23).

How has this happened?

Clever but carnal men learned how to manufacture revival-like results. Depending on psychological manipulation, and Madison Street marketing, false prophets have separated the Gospel from its biblical context, and repackaged it to be more palatable to the world. Repentance has been discarded, or redefined until it's meaningless, and Hell is rarely mentioned. And when it is, it has been so air-conditioned that no sinner smells its brimstone or feels its heat anymore. The Holy Ghost does not attend such preaching as that, and this is disastrous because it is the Holy Ghost alone Who is sent into the world to reprove the heart of sinners, and draw them to the Saviour. All who come to Jesus apart from this holy influence have no more hope of finding repentance than did Judas, or Esau.

How does this relate to fasting? If sinners will be genuinely converted, they must repent under the influence of the Holy Ghost, Who was sent into the world to reprove it of sin, righteousness and judgment. Jesus said His Spirit would flow through the belly of believers into the world around us. We need a movement of the Holy Ghost, and He moves through our belly. Until we humble ourselves by serious fasting and prayers, and surrender our belly to the control of the Holy Ghost, we will have no revival. The pretenders will continue to get away with dancing in their own fire, but it is not the Lord's fire (Leviticus 10:1). So we need the Holy Spirit's instruction for a fast that God will honor with the blessing promised in Isaiah 58:8-14.

The Israelites complained because God rejected their fast; but their fasting was insincere, and unserious (Isaiah 58:3-7).

Serious fasting requires that we set ourselves apart from our own pleasures and our own labor while we fast and pray (Isaiah 58:3). No TV, no movies, no golf, no comics, no sports page, no sports activities, no radio. You may not indulge yourself in any of the activities that you normally enjoy for pleasure's sake (I Corinthians 7:5). Nor may you "exact all your labours" (Isaiah 58:3). On this I must add some clarification.

God's complaint is specific, "(you) exact *all* (emphasis added) your labours." Ideally, we ought to separate ourselves from our labors during a fast. But this is not always possible or necessary. I am relieved that the Spirit allows for the performance of those tasks that are essential, or else many of us, mothers in particular, could rarely fast. Of course, some occupations may not allow for fasting while performing any of the tasks they demand; for example, when health or safety might be a concern (Matthew 15:32), or when an employer will likely be cheated by the reduced production of a fasting employee (I Timothy 6:1-2).

The Scriptural support for this observation is that Jesus would not have the multitude begin a long walk home while they were fasting, lest they should "faint in the way" (Matthew 15:32). On the other hand, there are professions that require some tasks which can be adequately addressed without compromising anyone's concern for health or safety, and, within reason, I think the Lord accepts such a fast unless the individual is insincere in his commitment to fasting and prayers and goes on *exacting all his labor*.

Jesus often ran up against the Pharisees' tendency to apply some of God's regulations beyond their intended application. For example, with regard to the Sabbath, the Pharisees insisted no work of any kind could be done without violating the Sabbath. Jesus rebuked them often for this mistake by doing His Father's works on the Sabbath day on purpose (Matthew 12:10-13; etc.). Jesus often pointed out that these hypocrites would free a sheep or an ox if it fell into a ditch on the Sabbath, yet they would accuse Jesus for healing on the Sabbath. Once, Jesus allowed His hungry disciples to pluck corn on the Sabbath (Matthew 12:1-9). The Pharisees jumped on this opportunity to accuse Jesus. But Jesus challenged them to apply that same rule to David when he and his men were hungry, and ate the shewbread, which was not lawful for them to eat (Matthew 12:4). He also pointed out that in the Old Testament, the priests worked on the sabbath days, and yet were blameless (Matthew 12:5). When you read Isaiah 58:3, notice that the Spirit's language is that we are not to *exact all our labors*.

Serious fasting requires a pure motive and purpose. We must not fast, "for strife and debate, and to smite with the fist of wickedness ... to make (our) voice to be heard on high" (Isaiah 58:4). Imagine God's children supposing that by fasting they can manipulate God to take sides with them against another. Imagine someone attempting to use fasting to get revenge. Imagine anyone so evil they would use fasting to advance some wicked purpose.

Fasting is not to be used in a fashion similar to how witches use magic, or hexes, or spells, summoning some force to manipulate the will of others to serve their interests. Like witches, some Christians think prayer and fasting is a weapon they can use to control others and further their own ambitions. The Spirit through Isaiah condemns fasting for selfish, sinful purposes in a manner similar to how the Spirit through James warned us our prayers will be ineffective if we pray to satisfy the lust of our flesh (James 4:3).

Serious fasting opens our heart to God's heart to loose the bands of wickedness and to undo the heavy burdens so that the oppressed may go free (Isaiah 58:6).

There are *bands of righteousness* and then there are *bands of wickedness* (Psalm 2:3; Isaiah 58:6). The *bands of righteousness* are the restraints against the wicked that are to be enforced by divinely appointed authorities (Romans 13:1-6). When the wicked rise in power and influence, these *bands* are broken, and the people are brought under the oppression of *bands of wickedness* that are forged in Hell. The sword (civil authority) that is given to punish evildoers and reward the righteous (Romans 13:4) is turned against the good, and in support of the evil. When this happens, it is necessary that believers fast and pray to loosen the bands of wickedness.

There are burdens heavy to be borne, strapped to our backs by cords of sin. On the other hand, there is that burden which is light, duties bound to us by the cords of the Gospel (Isaiah 58:6; Matthew 11:30). The wicked strive to break the cords that tether us to those duties that contribute to our felicity and prosperity (Proverbs 14:34). And in their place, they bind grievous burdens upon their backs with cords of sin. When this occurs, it is necessary that believers fast and pray to break the cords of sin and undo the heavy burdens.

Who has not lately heard the cry of the heathen in our own land, "Let us break their bands asunder, and cast away their cords from us" (Psalm 2:3)? We must cry out to God as did Israel in Egypt or we will be thrown into that furnace ourselves (Exodus 3:9). A fast that mourns the growing strength of the bands of wickedness in our land, a cry to God for the marvelous power of the Holy Ghost to break those bands of wickedness that bind upon you and your loved ones the evil burdens of sin, a fast that cries out to God on behalf of the oppressed in our own, and in every land, a fast that opens our heart to God's heart, that empties it of selfish desires so that He may fill it with His own — this is the fast the Lord seeks from us.

Serious fasting involves sincere repenting. The Prophet Isaiah instructed us that God seeks a fast that is accompanied by genuine repentance. We must break every yoke, deal our bread to the hungry, attend to the needs of the poor, and fulfill our obligations to our own families (I Timothy 5:8). Indeed, we must fast and pray and act in concert. The rest of Isaiah 58 through 59:19 speaks to the importance of genuine repentance accompanying our fasting and prayers.

But our hearts are hard, and they are cold, and our confession of sin must offend Him. Indeed! The Spirit through the Apostle Paul rebuked the Corinthian Christians, and they were made sorry, and that sorrow worked genuine repentance in their hearts. II Corinthians 7:11: "For ... ye sorrowed after a godly sort, what carefulness it wrought in you, yea, what clearing of yourselves, yea, what indignation, yea, what fear, yea, what vehement desire, yea, what zeal, yea, what revenge! In all things ye have approved yourselves to be clear in this matter." Here is repentance: passionate, serious, and sincere. Compare your own cold confession of sins to this and see that we desperately need fasting and praying to humble our lifted up soul, to soften our hardened hearts. O my friend, the failure of believers to obtain the promise of II Chronicles 7:14 is here — a failure to humble our souls that He might grant to us true repentance.

These phony revivals that sweep through town and make no difference, these evangelistic campaigns that sow naught but tares, these ministries overrun by dogs and goats, where genuine sheep are slaughtered, or starved, this nonsense that 76% of Americans are born again when it's obviously not true — it must stop! We must return to the formula of the Early Church, to preach "the gospel ... with the Holy Ghost sent down from heaven" (I Peter 1:12). Strong devils have deluded many otherwise good men, but there is a stirring, an awakening. These seducing spirits that have dulled the spiritual senses of so many by sleep are being challenged: challenged by men and women of God who are fasting and praying for revival. But we need more. We need you to join us. Fast and pray for revival. And when you fast, do it sincerely and seriously.

Something to think about:

1. Is it always appropriate to fast? Did Jesus anticipate that sometimes we would fast in public (Matthew 6:16-18)? What are some occasions when it would not be appropriate to fast?

2. Have you ever fasted hoping this would give you an advantage over others? Did it work out for you?

3. Have you ever fasted and felt you did not get the results you sought? Was anything said in this chapter that might help you understand why?

Chapter Four

Secret Fasting!

"First, let it (fasting) be done unto the Lord, with our eye singly fixed on Him. Let our intention herein be this, and this alone, to glorify our Father which is in heaven; to express our sorrow and shame for our manifold transgressions of His holy law; to wait for an increase of purifying grace, drawing our affections to things above; to add seriousness and earnestness to our prayers; to avert the wrath of God; and to obtain all the great and precious promises which He hath made to us in Jesus Christ."

– John Wesley

For this exercise, you will need a globe, a magnifying glass, a sewing needle, and a sanctified imagination. Find Israel on your globe. With your needle, make a small pinprick on Jerusalem. Suppose it's about 900 BC. With your magnifying glass, study the small cavity you made with the needle and imagine you are looking at the Temple of Solomon. Peer into the Temple, and peek behind the veil. Look for a gold covered wooden box called the Ark of the Covenant. The top of the Ark is called the *Mercy Seat.* Two cherubs, each stretching its wings toward the other, shadow the *Mercy Seat.* Concentrate on the empty space beneath the wings of the cherubim. You are now looking at the exclusive dwelling place of the Spirit of Almighty God in 900 BC, in a small room that He called the Holy Place. When the high priest presented the sacrifice before this Ark, God's glory filled the Temple. But when Israel was in disfavor with the Lord, the Holy Ghost did not fill the Temple.

Skip forward 900 years. It's the last day of the Feast of Tabernacles. The priests have poured out the water that rushes across the Temple floor and down into the streets of Jerusalem, commemorating the spring of waters God gave to Israel by the hand of Moses when he smote the rock in the wilderness. Standing in up to three inches of water, Jesus cried, "If any man thirst, let him come unto me, and drink. He that believeth on me, as the scripture hath said, out of his belly shall flow rivers of living water" (John 7:37-38). Jesus was talking about the coming of the Holy Spirit, which had not yet been given, because Jesus had not yet been glorified (John 7:39). This *glorification* refers to His death, burial, and resurrection.

The Scripture tells us that Christ is that Rock (I Corinthians 10:4). And the waters that flowed from it represented the coming of the Holy Spirit of God into the world through Jesus Christ after His crucifixion. Jesus invited us to drink of this water. And He promised that this water (the Holy Spirit) would flow through the belly of all who believe. The Lord has claimed our body and decreed it to be the temple of God (I Corinthians 6:19-20). The earthly dwelling place of the Spirit of God is no longer limited to that itty-bitty spot beneath the wings of the cherubim on the *Mercy Seat*. Instead, He dwells in the hearts of all who believe on Jesus Christ (Galatians 4:6). And Jesus expects the Holy Ghost to flow from our belly like a river of living water. Capture the vision: millions of believers, all over the world, each one the temple of God, where God dwells in the New Testament *holy place*, and through whom the Holy Ghost will flow into the world. We saw it in the early days of the Lord's churches, the Holy Ghost flowing mightily, powerfully, fully, and gloriously. But now we are amazed when we see trickles. Now we must sing, "Mercy drops 'round us are falling, but for the showers we plead." Why?

If you are a believer, you are a priest in the New Testament temple (I Peter 2:5), which is your body (I Corinthians 6:19-20), and your heart is His holy place (Galatians 4:6). It's a royal priesthood, charged with the duty of presenting spiritual sacrifices (I Peter 2:5). God has invested this treasure in earthen vessels (II Corinthians 4:7). And so He commands His priests to study how to keep their vessels in sanctification and honor (I Thessalonians 4:4; compare II Timothy 2:21). Many of the vessels are unsanctified. Covetous, corrupt priests have defiled the temple of God. These priests grieve the Spirit (Ephesians 4:30-31) and even quench Him (I Thessalonians 5:19). And so *the glory is departed* (I Samuel 4:21), and the river does not flow.

Many New Testament priests today are like Hophni

and Phinehas, the sons of Eli (I Samuel 1-3). They were belly-servers, feeding their own lusts (I Samuel 2:12-17). These wicked priests "lay with the women that assembled at the door of the Tabernacle of the congregation" (I Samuel 2:22). God destroyed them. You are Christ's priests today. Do you erect idols of covetousness in the very room where the Holy Ghost dwells (Colossians 3:5)? Do you entertain impure thoughts in the very throne room of the Father's Holy Spirit? Do you commit adultery and fornication in your heart (Matthew 5:28)? Consider that your heart is the holy of holies of the New Testament temple. If God destroyed Old Testament priests for these things, of how much greater judgment do you suppose such New Testament priests are worthy?

The *rivers* will not flow until these wicked priests repent. And the priests will not repent until they are humbled. And they will be humbled! God is going to move mightily in our midst and purge His House (I Timothy 3:15). The priests who refuse to repent will be destroyed (I Corinthians 3:17). Fellow priests, if we judge ourselves, we may avert the coming judgment of God (I Corinthians 11:31). Mark my words! Judgment is framed in the heart of God, and when it begins, those who are of the spirit of Hophni and Phinehas will drop dead in our churches as did Ananias and Sapphira (Acts 5). So I call upon you to humble your soul with fasting (Psalm 35:13). And in this article, I address the issue of secrecy.

Fasting is for heavenly glow, not earthly show. Jesus expressly forbad us to follow the example of the hypocrites (Matthew 6:16-19). They fasted to be seen of men. They did it for show. We are to fast for our Heavenly Father, to receive His honor, to enjoy the glow of His favor upon our lives. For that reason, Jesus instructed us to avoid putting on the long face, so as to appear unto men to be fasting.

But there is confusion over the principle of secrecy in fasting. Some have mistakenly taken Jesus' words in Matthew 6:16-19 as instructing us to tell no one when we are fasting. Of course, that is absurd on the face of it. The Apostle Paul instructed couples to not abstain from one another in the marriage bed except with one another's consent, for the purpose of fasting (I Corinthians 7:5; see Hebrews 13:4). Obviously, the Holy Ghost expected married couples to agree together on seasons of fasting and that involves letting someone know. We also have examples of publicly called fasts (Esther 4:16; see also Joel 1:14; 2:15). The disciples often fasted together; and therefore, they were not fasting secretly (Acts 13:3; 14:23). The instruction to avoid fasting in order to be seen of men does not require that you keep the fact that you are fasting a secret. The mistake is owing to a misreading of the text.

Jesus did not tell us to be secretive about our fasting. He told us that the Father is the One Who is "in secret." He is invisible to our physical eyes, and He watches us "in secret." It does not say you are to be secretive in your fasting; it says that we are fasting for Him Who is invisible (Hebrews 11:27), who watches in secret. And we are to do this anticipating a public demonstration of His favor (blessedness) upon our lives. What we are not to do is to fast for the favor of men.

It is not a violation of Jesus' words concerning fasting to inform your spouse, family, and even your friends when you are entering into a season of fasting and prayers. It might be necessary in some instances, in order to avoid unnecessarily offending someone with your otherwise inexplicable behavior, such as avoiding invitations to dine, otherwise inexplicable physical weakness, difficulty concentrating, and so on. There are times when you might enter into a covenant to fast with other brothers or sisters in Christ (Acts 13:3; 14:23). There are times when you might be called upon to participate in a church-wide fast (Esther 4:16). And there may be times when you inform only those who must know. Being sensitive to Jesus' instruction to avoid fasting in order to garner the favor of men ought to motivate us to be careful about our motivation regarding who is informed about our fast, but it does not require us to keep it a secret.

All believers who fear that America is overdue for judgment (Jeremiah 9:9) need to remember that He begins with the House of God (I Peter 4:17 with I Timothy 3:15). He warned us that those priests who defile the temple of God would be destroyed (I Corinthians 3:17; I Peter 2:5; Revelation 1:5-6; with I

Corinthians 6:19-20). Are you a faithful priest in the temple of God? Will you present the sacrifice of intercessory prayer for America (Psalm 141:2)? Will you humble yourself, and pray, and seek His face (II Chronicles 7:14)? Will you humble your soul with fasting (Psalm 35:13)? And when you do, take care you fast seriously, sincerely, and for the glory of our Father Who watches in secret, desiring to reward you openly.

Something to think about:

1. What is the role of fasting relative to the moving of God's Spirit through our lives?

2. Are we supposed to keep our fasting a secret from everybody? Why, or why not? Do you agree with the author's explanation of Matthew 6:16-19 with regard to secret fasting?

3. Were you impressed by a sense of urgency regarding your role as a priest in God's temple? Have you been a faithful priest?

4. What changes need to take place in your life, and how might fasting with prayer help you make these changes?

Chapter Five

The Three Most Famous Fasts

"We should fast when we are concerned for God's work. I believe the greatest thing a church could have is a staff, deacons, and leaders who fast and pray – not when the church burns down, but in order to get the church on fire. … Fasting brings about a supernatural work in our lives."

– Charles Stanley

"**O**ne nation under God" is still in our pledge, though many Christians think it should not be. I am not among them. While there has been a great deal of movement in this country away from our spiritual heritage, the answer is not to give in. We should never give place to the Devil (Ephesians 4:27). A return to the God Who created all men equal, and granted to every man certain unalienable rights is what is needed. George Washington was a man of profound faith in the Sovereign God of nations. When reflecting on the prospects of war with Britain for American independence he wrote these words in his general orders to his men, on July 2, 1776: "… The fate of unborn millions will now depend, *under God,* on the courage and conduct of this army."[1] At Gettysburg, Abraham Lincoln echoed this foundational principle when he said, "that this nation, *under God,* shall have a new birth of freedom."[2] (emphasis added) Let no one tell you that the idea that America is one nation under God is something lately contrived and forced into the pledge by religious zealots in the mid-fifties. On the other hand, don't suppose for a moment this country can remain one nation under God unless He grants us a new spiritual awakening.

I have shown from the Scripture that Jesus expects us to fast in these days (Mark 2:20). I don't have to convince you that Satan is actively seeking whom he may devour (I Peter 5:8), that he sometimes hinders our work (I Thessalonians 2:18), and that we must resist him (James 4:7). Indeed, Scripture promises that if we resist the Devil, he will flee from us. But the context of that verse requires that we first submit to God. No one who refuses to accept the clear teaching of the Bible on the subject of fasting should pretend he has sufficient power with God to resist the Devil, for he is clearly insubordinate to Christ Jesus. Jesus said there are devils that can be overcome only by prayer and fasting (Matthew 17:21), and it seems increasingly clear to me that many of His churches are hindered by devils of this kind.

After Easter, each year, our church enters into a period of fasting and prayers for forty days. As I write this, one or more of our members is fasting and praying for revival. I have a preaching engagement next week, but when I return, I'll enter into an extended period of fasting and praying for many things of concern to me, but over and above all, I'll be praying for a revival of God's people in America. For, the last nation under God in history was Judah, and we all know what happened to that nation when it turned away from the God of their fathers. It is more than coincidence that the very nations God used to judge Judah are rattling their sabers at America today. Selah!

In this article, I want to encourage you to begin a study of the famous fasts in the Bible. The most famous are the forty-days fasts of Jesus, Moses, and Elijah. After that, I suppose either Daniel's twenty-one days fast, or Esther's three days fast would qualify as among the most well known. For the purpose of these articles, however, we will concentrate on the most famous fast of all—the forty-days fast of the Lord Jesus Christ.

Toward the end of His earthly ministry, Jesus met with Elijah and Moses in what Peter called the *holy mount* (II Peter 1:18; See Matthew 17:1-9; Mark 9:2-10; Luke 9:28-36). In the presence of Peter, James, and John, the Father exalted His only begotten Son above Moses and Elijah; at the same time, He showed to us whom He has chosen to sit beside His Son in His Kingdom (Matthew 20:21; Zechariah 4:14). These three are noteworthy for being the most spiritually empowered men who ever walked on earth, Jesus Christ being greatest among them, to Whom the Father gave not His Spirit by measure (John 3:34).[3] Something else connects these three. Each of them is noteworthy for having fasted forty days and forty nights (*Moses,*

44

twice – Deuteronomy 9:9-19 in Mt. Horeb; *Elijah* – I Kings 19:8 in Mt. Horeb, here called the *mount of God*; *Jesus, the Christ* – Matthew 4:1-11; Luke 4:1-14, led "up" of the Spirit into the wilderness).[4] The Spirit intended for us to make the connection between the power these men demonstrated and their fasting and prayers in this *holy mount.* But in case you're among those reduced from "ears" (Matthew 11:15) to "an ear" (Revelation 2:7), and so suffer from some dullness of hearing (Hebrews 5:11), the Spirit makes this connection very clear in what occurred after they came down from the *holy mount.*

Peter, James, and John, returned with Jesus to the other disciples after the most glorious mountain top experience in Christian history. And, immediately, they were presented with the case of the child possessed with a demon the disciples were powerless to cast out (Matthew 17:14-21), even though Jesus had before given them power over *all devils* (Luke 9:1). Jesus lamented, "O faithless and perverse generation, how long shall I be with you? how long shall I suffer you? bring him hither to me" (Matthew 17:17). Jesus then rebuked the devil, and "the child was cured from that very hour." Ashamed, they asked why they could not cast out this devil. Jesus explained that it was because of their unbelief, and exposed how little was their faith. But then He said, "Howbeit this kind goeth not out but by prayer and fasting" (Matthew 17:21). If any continue to have trouble seeing the clear connection between fasting with prayers and the demonstration of the power of God (I Thessalonians 1:5), all I can say is, apparently, it is not for them to know the mysteries of the Kingdom of Heaven (Matthew 13:11).

We notice that when Jesus returned from His desert fast, the Spirit specifically declared that He "returned in the power of the Spirit" (Luke 4:14). But Jesus already was filled with the Holy Ghost when He entered into the desert (Luke 4:1). Indeed, He was conceived by the power of the Holy Ghost (Luke 1:35). Yea, verily, the Word, being in the "form of God, thought it not robbery to be equal with God" (John 1:1; Philippians 2:5-9), and the Spirit of the Heavenly Father is none other than the Spirit of Christ (Romans 8:9). So, why did the Spirit point out particularly that, when Jesus returned from His forty days and nights of fasting and praying, He returned in the power of the Spirit? It is because the Spirit intends that we follow in His steps, and so desires us to know the path to power with God is in this example of His Son (I Peter 2:21).

Although we know the Apostles regularly fasted with prayers, we have no record that any of them fasted forty days. I think it would be ill conceived for any to presume to attempt it unless the Holy Spirit very specifically required it, for only then could anyone hope to be sustained through such a fast. Notice, in the case of Moses, Elijah, and Jesus, the Spirit compelled them. He directed when it was to begin, how long it was to continue, and exactly when it was to conclude.

Jesus has given us power (Acts 1:8). Indeed, greater is He that is in us, than he that is in the world. And like the father who brought his demon-possessed child to the disciples in hopes they could help him, fathers and mothers bring to us their sons and daughters in hopes we might help them against the demons that assault their lives. Believe me when I say they don't need more activities for their children, and they certainly don't need us to accommodate the demons that already have control of their flesh through their carnal music and dress and attitudes of rebellion. What they need is to come to a church where there are men of God who have the power of God on their lives sufficient to address the demons that plague their families. And the kind of demons attacking our kids today, brethren, are the kind that require fasting and prayers to overcome.

Something to think about:

1. What does it mean if we refuse to fast and pray?

2. What shows that there is a direct relationship between fasting with prayers and open demonstrations of the power of God's Kingdom in the world today?

3. Does your church provide a public demonstration of the power of God? Or does it sparkle and spit like static electricity, but lacks the full current of Holy Ghost power? How can fasting with prayers help secure the full current of Kingdom power for your church?

Chapter Six

The Saviour's Fast (Part One) — Invited Into The Holy Place

"Fasting is important–more important, perhaps than many of us have supposed … it's not a major biblical doctrine, a foundation stone of the faith, or a panacea for every spiritual ill. Nevertheless, when exercised with a pure heart and a right motive, fasting may provide us with a key to unlock doors where other keys have failed; a window opening up new horizons in the unseen world; a spiritual weapon of God's providing, 'mighty to the pulling down of strongholds.'"

– Arthur Wallis

We've been invited (Hebrews 4:16)! So come with me into the throne room of the Almighty (Revelation 4-5).

Heaven's doors open and our eyes are immediately stabbed with spears of light so bright we're blinded. Undulating from deep within the brilliant room are sounds that wash over us like waves so pure we neither of us dare to cry out, or even to whisper. Suddenly, a thunderous roar reverberates in the air. Fear crawls, no claws, across our flesh exciting a sense of self-loathing and an intense foreboding that we don't belong in this place. At just the moment we begin to withdraw, our joints go loose and we find ourselves whisked deep into the room, and now we are lying prostrate on its floor, before a sea of glass like crystal. There is the sound of fluttering wings over our heads, and the sensation of a balm anointing our eyes, and the sweet cooing of a dove. Peace passing understanding settles us as our eyes begin to focus on the glorious sights in this holy place.

Firelight flashes and sparkles in the sea of glass like crystal spraying us with shafts of brilliant light and setting aglow the mirror like floor below us. We did not stand ourselves up upon this floor, but we find ourselves standing there nonetheless, agog at the sight of the great throne before us. A glance is all we can bear, but from that single glance, burned in our brain is the image of a fiery throne, and one sitting in it with a face shining in the brightness of the noonday sun, over arched by an emerald rainbow, with lightening streaking to and from the throne in every direction. Intermittent thunder roars so deep and powerful that but for whatever invisible grace sustains us in this place, we would instantly surely turn to dust and ashes. The sound of many waters swells behind us and when we turn, there we see a Lamb, as it had been slain. Suddenly, we sense we have been released from the grip of an invisible and irresistible force. Instinctively, we know the only safe place for us is by the Lamb; so we flee to Him and cling to Him with all the strength remaining in us.

Consider brethren, we have been called to come boldly into this place — this room where God sits upon His throne, surrounded by the four beasts and the twenty-four elders, and where the cherubim repeat "Holy, holy, holy, Lord God Almighty, which was, and is, and is to come" (Revelation 4:8) while the seraphim weave their own glorious melody around the holy refrain — how can we come boldly into this room? Behold the Lamb in the midst of the throne: our welcome here is owing to His invitation. And why has He invited us to enter His heavenly tabernacle? It is to find grace to help in time of need.

Remember the daddy with the demon-possessed child crying for help from the men of God? Come, brethren, come mothers and fathers, come preachers and deacons and Sunday school teachers and Christian school teachers, come to the throne of grace where you may obtain mercy and find that grace to help in time of need.

What has this to do with fasting? The flesh has no place before the throne of Almighty God. Fasting gets the flesh out of the way.

In Exodus 20:26, Moses was moved by the Holy Spirit to write, "Neither shalt thou go up by steps unto mine altar, that thy nakedness be not discovered thereon." Did the bare ankles of a man bring a blush to God's face — of course not! These things are written for our admonition, specifically, for those of us "upon whom the ends of the world are come" (I Corinthians

10:11). Who with New Testament light regarding the irreconcilable enmity that separates the flesh of man from God, cannot see the point of this instruction (Romans 8:7)? Yea, God would not have a flash of flesh in His presence. We must worship Him in "spirit and in truth." Those in the *flesh* need not bother (Romans 8:8). But we are not in the flesh, but in the Spirit, if so be that the Spirit of God dwell in us (Romans 8:9). Let us therefore "walk in the Spirit" (Galatians 5:16), and not after the flesh (Romans 8:1-4), particularly when we come to pray before the throne of the Almighty God. Beware you do not show a flash of flesh in His presence, lest He immediately close the doors of His countenance against you and refuse to hear you (Isaiah 59:1-2; James 4:3 with I John 2:16; Galatians 5:16).

By fasting we weaken the hold of the appetites of our flesh on our spirit; yea, we humble our lifted up soul; yea, we bring this body under, and allow our spirit to embrace the grace, the thrice holy grace of the Lover, the Helper, the Healer of our sin-sickened souls. Fasting slaps proud fleshly appetite and rebuffs its constant demand for preeminence over spiritual ones. 'Tis strange how spiritual hunger increases with physical hunger, and how when physical hunger is denied its demands, spiritual hunger turns fully to God and is fed that sweet heavenly manna till it is full of the glory of the Lord, and His righteousness (Matthew 5:6).

The forty-days fasts of our Lord Jesus, and His

servants, Moses and Elijah, are the most famous fasts in history. We will focus on the greatest of these — the forty-days fast of Jesus our Lord.

The forty-days fast of Jesus is recorded in Matthew 4 and Luke 4. We must consider both accounts to get the complete picture. The Spirit, by the beloved physician, Luke, testifies that Jesus already was "full of the Holy Ghost" before He followed the Spirit into the desert (Luke 4:1). Indeed, in Him has dwelt the fullness of the Godhead bodily from the moment of conception (Colossians 2:9; Philippians 2:5-11; I Timothy 3:16; Luke 1:35). Matthew tells us He was "led up of the Spirit," indicating two things: first, that He went up, probably into a desert mountain, sequestered from the daily routine of His life, secluded from the world, alone with God. And second, this He did under the influence and direction of the Holy Spirit.

Sometimes the Spirit leads us into an extended fast sequestered from family and friends. Later, I offer insight to help you discern when the Spirit is calling you to such a fast. It is certain that some will be shocked to learn how often the Spirit called for such a fast but was not followed "into the desert."

The Spirit, by Luke, informs us that throughout the forty days of fasting, Jesus was tempted of the Devil (Luke 4:2). This helps us unravel a knot concerning these two accounts. We find that the order of the temptation recorded in Luke (stone to bread, kneel to

Satan, leap from the pinnacle) differs from that given in Matthew 4 (stone to bread, leap from pinnacle, kneel to Satan). We also note that in Luke's account the Spirit reveals that Jesus said to Satan, "Get thee behind me, Satan" (Luke 4:8), but in the Apostle Matthew's account we are told He said, "Get thee hence, Satan" (Matthew 4:10). Clearly, sometime during the course of Jesus' forty days of fasting, Satan assaulted Him, first tempting Him to turn the stone to bread, next, perhaps even some few days later, tempting Him to bow down and worship Satan, and finally, again, perhaps some days later still, attacking Him with the temptation to leap from the pinnacle. At this effort, Jesus, knowing his battle was not yet done, commanded Satan not to depart, but to take the place that belonged to him, behind the Son of God. But when the forty days of fasting was completed, Satan unleashed upon Him one final assault, and that is what we find recorded in the Apostle Matthew's account. When this was finished, Jesus commanded Satan to depart.

In the next article, we'll explore insights from the example of our Lord Jesus Christ into the work the Holy Spirit desires to accomplish in our hearts during an extended period of fasting and prayers.

Something to think about:

1. Were you transported into the throne room of the Almighty as you read through the opening paragraphs of this chapter? Read through Revelation 4-5 and from

the Spirit's description of Heaven, use your mind to construct in your heart a clear picture of this holy place and let it become your prayer closet.

2. In what way does fasting prepare us to move into the presence of God? What specific issues does it address?

3. Have you ever fasted for a period of two or more days? If you have, do you remember Satan taking advantage of your weakness to assault you with manifold temptations? Meditate upon Jesus' battle with temptation during His forty-days fast and jot down some insights that will help you the next time you encounter such temptations.

4. Have you noticed that Luke's account of the wilderness temptation of Christ places Satan's effort to get Jesus to bow down to him second, while that temptation is listed third in the Apostle Matthew's account? What do you think of the author's explanation of this?

Chapter Seven

The Saviour's Fast (Part Two) — Battling Temptation During Prayer And Fasting

"I often felt myself weak in the presence of temptation and needed frequently to hold days of fasting and prayer … to retain that communion with God and that hold upon the Divine truth that would enable me efficiently to labor for the promotion of revivals of religion."

– Charles G. Finney

What a wonderful meeting we have had with Brother Beckum this past week (January 14, 2008)! God moved mightily, our people were blessed, and our church revived. During one of his messages, he mentioned that the human body would die after seven days without water. I did some research and discovered that the consensus is that a person will die of dehydration after anywhere from three to seven days, depending on factors like health, and level of activity during the abstinence.[5] I mention this here for two reasons. First, to alert you to the importance of being wise and circumspect regarding extended periods of fasting, and second, because a while back, I fasted for fourteen days, and the first seven of those days I took neither food nor drink, and lived to tell about it.

Occasionally, I become so overwhelmed by a sense of God's displeasure toward His people, and foreboding of imminent judgment, that I am driven to extended periods of fasting and prayer for revival. The fourteen-days fast mentioned above was one of those occasions. I had determined I would neither eat nor drink until the Lord bid me *come and dine*. On the seventh day, it came to my mind that I should begin taking some water. I was unaware that it was the consensus of nutritionists that one would die of dehydration after three to seven days without water, so now I find it very interesting that the Lord impressed upon me the need to take some water on the seventh day of that fast. However, at that time, I was skeptical that I was merely surrendering to weakness of the flesh. I prayed about it and discussed it with my wife. Of course, she greatly desired me to take some water. After more prayer, I became convinced it was the Lord, so I waited until near the end of the seventh day, and began taking a little water. I continued my fast for seven more days, slowly introducing more and more water, and finally, believing the Lord had bid me *come and dine,* I broke my fast after fourteen days.

Our current topic is the forty-days fast of Jesus, our Lord. One of the main points I hope to make in this article is the importance that we, like Jesus, are led up of the Spirit into any extended periods of fasting. That is the first insight I offer from Jesus' forty-days fast. He was "led up of the Spirit" into this extended fast.

We must be sensitive to the leading of the Holy Spirit in everything we do, and this is nowhere more important than in an extended fast (three or more days).

Jesus was led up of the Spirit into the wilderness "to be tempted of the devil" (Matthew 4:1). Jesus taught us to pray, "lead us not into temptation" (Matthew 6:13). Why did the Spirit lead Jesus into the wilderness to be tempted of the Devil?

This question is especially important in view of the fact that the Bible says, "God cannot be tempted with evil, neither tempteth he any man" (James 1:13). Thomas knelt before Jesus and cried, "my Lord and my God" (John 20:28) and was not reproved, for he spoke the truth concerning Jesus our Lord (John 1:1,14; Colossians 1:15-18; Hebrews 1:3, 8-9; Philippians 2:5-11). If Jesus is God, and God cannot be tempted, how is it that Jesus was led of the Spirit into the wilderness to be tempted of the Devil?

We cannot say that while He was led up to be tempted, in fact He was not tempted, for the Holy Ghost has testified that He was indeed tempted (Hebrews 4:15).

Finally, what has this to do with prayer and fasting?

First, let's address the question of how it is that Jesus was "in all points tempted like as we are, yet without sin" (Hebrews 4:15).

No believer would resist the Spirit's witness to the

spotless Lamb of God, and so the difficulty is not that Jesus was "yet without sin." The difficulty comes with the Spirit's testimony that He was "tempted like as we are." The reason that presents a difficulty to us is that the Holy Ghost has defined temptation as occurring when a man is "drawn away of his own lust, and enticed" (James 1:14).

The "enticed" part is no problem. Clearly, Satan attempted to entice Jesus into disobedience to His Father during his temptation in the wilderness. The question comes down to this; how was Jesus "drawn away of His own lust"?

Jesus has lusts? The word *lust* refers to a strong appetite. We tend to think of it in terms of sexual sins, but the word *lust* is used in the Bible to speak of appetites that God encourages His people to feed (Deuteronomy 12:15-21; 14:26). Certainly, it is true that our sinful flesh craves, or lusts, for unholy, and ungodly things, and the Holy Spirit is contrary to the flesh, and so lusts against it (Galatians 5:17). Yes, God has strong appetites; but His appetites are for righteousness, mercy, judgment, justice, godliness, purity, goodness, and whatever might not misbecome our Mighty God.

When Jesus came looking for fruit upon a fig tree, and cursed it when He found none (Matthew 21:19), it was symbolic. The fig tree is used to represent Israel and its fruit represents her character (Jeremiah 24:1-8;

see also Hosea 9:10; Joel 1:7 and Luke 13:7 with 21:29). He came to His fig tree, hungry for its fruit, the precious fruit of righteousness (James 3:18) expected from a repentant heart (Matthew 3:8). He found none (Romans 3:10-23)! Provoked, He cursed the tree. It brings to mind the shameful day that first Adam used its leaves to hide his shame from his Maker. Indeed, Jesus hungers and thirsts for righteousness (Matthew 5:6).

Jesus was not drawn away by a lust for evil. The Holy Ghost says God cannot be tempted with evil (James 1:13). Therefore it is clear that those verses that tell us Israel tempted God (Psalm 78:18-56; 95:8-9; 106:14; see Exodus 17:2-7; Numbers 14:22; Deuteronomy 6:16), cannot be understood to mean they *tempted Him with evil.* What they did to tempt Him was evil, but God was not drawn away and enticed by their evil to join them in it. He was tempted, however, to execute upon them the judgment they deserved for their foolhardy behavior. In the New Testament, the Holy Ghost warns us not to follow the example of these Israelites in the wilderness: "Neither let us tempt Christ, as some of them also tempted, and were destroyed of serpents" (I Corinthians 10:9; see also Acts 15:10).[6] Since we are warned against tempting Him, we know it must be possible. However, it is not possible to *tempt* Christ with evil, because there is nothing in evil that could appeal to Him. How did Satan tempt the Lord?

Did you notice that each temptation was an effort to draw Jesus away by His strong desire to honor His

Heavenly Father? Turn the stone to bread, he said, not to feed your starved belly, but to prove you are the Son of God. Leap from the Temple tower, Satan hissed, and validate the truthfulness of the Word of Your Heavenly Father. There is no question that validating His Father's Word and His Own identity as His Father's Son were strong motivations in Jesus, but Satan failed to seduce Jesus into sin by these temptations.

Satan would try another tactic. For God so loved the world that He gave His only begotten Son, not to judge the world, but that the world might be saved from Satan's power through Him (John 3:16-17; Acts 26:18). The Devil dangled a tempting proposition before this Son, and heir. He would willingly hand over to Jesus all the kingdoms of the world. All Jesus would have to do is to kneel before Satan, and worship him.

Before you dismiss this as an absurd attempt on the part of Satan, consider that Jesus was fully aware of the price He would pay to save the world from Satan's power (John 3:16). Visit Gethsemene, and watch with Him for at least one hour, agonizing over the prospect of Calvary as He prayed, sweating drops of blood, "Not my will, but thine." Enter into the prayer closet of the prophet David, in Psalm 22, and hear the Saviour crying from the Cross, in travail of soul so intense it rent the rocks beneath it. Now come into David's prayer closet again, at Psalm 18, and, transported by faith into the throne room of God (Revelation 4-5), hug the neck of the slain but living Lamb that stands before the throne there. Then watch as the Father watched His Son upon that Cross. Tremble with me as you see that, when His Son cried to Him from the Cross, He blew from His nostrils a smoke that billowed from Heaven and darkened the skies of earth. Gasp in awe of the awful stream of fire that shot from the mouth of God and ignited the coals on the altar before His throne, and then follow that blazing stream across the heavens to where it set ablaze that Lake of Fire. Fall prostrate before Him shaking as you're reading how His voice thundered out across the heavens in rage against the wicked as they crucified His Son. Only when you have seen the Cross, from the heart of the Father and of the Son, can you fully appreciate the marvel, the wonder that Jesus did so unhesitatingly turn down the crown that Satan offered to Him, and clung to the Cross His Father gave to Him instead. Now you can appreciate the triumph of the moment, so now hear Him say, "Get thee hence, Satan."

Next we will consider what this encounter meant to the ministry of our Saviour. The insights we will glean can have a profound impact on our ministry also. Because Jesus taught us that before you can spoil the strongman's house you must bind him, we know the strongman can be bound, and his house can be spoiled.

Something to think about:

1. What is an important caution to all who would enter into extended fasts?

2. Temptation is common to us all. Why can we have confidence that Jesus can relate to us when we are tempted?

3. We learned that *lust* does not refer only to sinful desires. What strong desires for good has Satan attempted to use to tempt you into sin?

Chapter Eight

The Saviour's Fast (Part Three) — Prayer And Fasting Prepares Us To Fulfill God's Plan

"Is not the neglect of this plain duty – I mean fasting, ranked by our Lord with almsgiving and prayer – one general occasion of deadness among Christians? Can any one willingly neglect it, and be guiltless?"

– John Wesley (1703-1791)

Jesus was *led of the Spirit* into the desert where He fasted forty days and nights. When I was a child, my dad would take the family with him to a place called Desert Dry Lake, in California. He built a flying machine, called a gyrocopter, and we went to the desert to enjoy tenting, and trail biking, and watching dad fly his "whirly bird" (his home–made flying machine). Often we lay side by side on the desert floor looking up into the brilliantly lit desert night sky, counting falling stars, and talking about the constellations. He taught me how to use the Big Dipper to find the North Star. He taught me how to find Orion's Belt, and to use the Belt to locate Canis Major and Taurus. He loved to talk about Orion, always reminding me that it figured prominently in the Bible and, he believed, it was the doorway into Heaven. Dad went home to Heaven two summers ago (2006). Now he knows whether his theory was correct. I often think of my time with my dad in the desert when reflecting on the forty days and nights Jesus spent with His heavenly Father there. Of course, the circumstances were very different. Jesus was *led of the Spirit* into the desert "to be tempted of the devil" (Matthew 4:1). However, in at least one way, Jesus' time in the desert with His Father and my time with my earthly father are similar. In both cases, a *father* was preparing his *son* for what was ahead.

Our Saviour has made clear the role of prayer in preparing us for what is coming. Regarding our readiness for His own return, He warned us to watch and pray (Mark 13:33; Luke 21:36). Jesus desired to prepare His disciples for His crucifixion, and for the great temptation that would come upon them to scatter when the Good Shepherd was smitten (Matthew 26:31; see Zechariah 13:7). He exhorted them to *watch and pray* as a way to protect them from entering into the temptation. The ordeal was foreordained and would come, and Satan would take every advantage to draw away His disciples, but if only they would *watch and pray,* they could avoid *entering* into that temptation. Earlier, on that portentous night, Peter had been warned that he would deny the Lord three times before the cock would crow. Jesus prayed for him, that his faith would not fail (Luke 22:32). Nevertheless, it was also necessary for Peter to pray. "And He cometh, and findeth them sleeping, and saith unto Peter, Simon, sleepest thou? couldest not thou watch one hour? Watch ye and pray, lest ye enter into temptation" (Mark 14:37-38a). How would Peter prepare for the coming *temptation*? It would be by prayer. (Prayer prepares us for what is coming. Who can tell what temptations Satan has planned for you today. You had better prepare by prayer. You had better keep your *one-hour watch*.) The Son of God prepared for the trial of His temptation by practicing what He preached. He completed His final preparations for the Cross by going into the Garden of Gethsemane to *watch and pray*.

Jesus' desert vigil was about more than merely testing, or proving Him. He was led into the desert to be tempted *of the devil,* Satan, called *the tempter,* God's enemy (Matthew 4:3; I Thessalonians 3:5; see Matthew 13:39). Indeed, it was the first front–line assault on Satan's kingdom of darkness by the Light of the world (John 8:12).

Satan's kingdom of darkness was a grand dominion, encompassing all the kingdoms of this world (Matthew 4:8-10; Luke 4:5-8), and Jesus meant to challenge Satan's claim on them. This desert sortie of the Son of God into Satan's territory was the opening salvo of that war for the souls of men that would end on the Cross, with Satan defeated, and Jesus rising from the dead, proclaiming, "All power is given unto me in heaven and in earth" (Mathew 28:18).

Jesus had come to spoil the strongman's *house* (kingdom), and who does not know that "One cannot enter into a strong man's house, and spoil his goods, except he first bind the strong man" (Matthew 12:29; see Mark 3:27). Jesus was *led of the Spirit into the desert to be tempted of the devil* because it was necessary that He first bind the strongman of the house in preparation to spoil his goods.

In an earlier article, I showed that, according to Jesus, certain kinds of devils cannot be cast out except by *prayer and fasting* (Matthew 17:21; Mark 9:29). The case that served as the occasion for this important lesson was a father who sought healing for his son who was lunatic (Matthew 17:15). However, Jesus was away, in the mountain, where He rendezvoused with Moses and Elijah, and was transfigured before Peter, James, and John, from His earthly form, into that heavenly glory He enjoyed with the Father before the world was (John 17:5; see Philippians 2:5-11 and John 1:1-14), then back again (Matthew 17:1-13). The nine disciples, awaiting their return, tried but could not deliver the child.[7] When Jesus arrived from the mountain, the father came and, kneeling before Him, implored Him to have mercy upon his son. After Jesus rebuked them all for their lack of faith, and perversity, He rebuked the devil too, and the child was "cured from that very hour" (Matthew 17:18). The disciples were perplexed, not because Jesus could, so easily, drive the devil away, but that they could not. For Jesus had given to them power over unclean spirits, and they were accustomed to devils fleeing from before them

(Matthew 10:1; see Luke 10:20). They asked Him why they could not deliver the child from the devil that possessed him. Jesus answered that it was because of their unbelief, and then added the insight that is vital to our understanding of spiritual warfare: "Howbeit this kind goeth not out but by prayer and fasting" (Matthew 17:21).

All of this raises questions. First, how is it that a devil can possess a child or a man? Second, how does prayer and fasting serve to break the power of the devil over the possessed man?

Satan is territorial (Revelation 2:13). He takes possession, occupies place, and exerts his will and power over what he controls (Luke 4:6; see Acts 26:18). However, he has no power over any territory until God grants it (Romans 13:1-6).[8] Satan presents his accusations against man before the throne of God (Revelation 12:10), and if his accusations are justified, God gives the Devil access to man's territory.

One example of this is the case of Peter, mentioned earlier. Jesus declared that the accuser, Satan, petitioned the throne of God for permission to sift him as wheat (Luke 22:31-32). The petition was granted.

On what basis, or by what accusation, did Satan gain this access to Peter? We do not know. Perhaps Peter's self-reliance, and failure to rightly understand the Cross made him vulnerable, or perhaps it is a circumstance like that of Job (Job 1-2). Nevertheless, this illustrates the point I'm making. Devils (spirits that serve Satan) occupy territory granted to Satan by God.

When we contemplate the horror of a child being possessed by a devil, we are particularly disturbed. Yet, we understand that sin and the evil it brings into the world afflicts not only those guilty of the trespass, but it also victimizes many who are innocent of the trespass. The simple example of the mother who uses drugs while pregnant, thus afflicting the child with her addiction, comes to mind. We are glad that those children who have at least one believing parent are holy, set apart to God (I Corinthians 7:14).

As to the second question, how does prayer and fasting serve to break the power of a devil over his territory, consider. Whenever Jesus did any miracle, virtue moved through him into the world (Luke 6:19; 8:46). The word that is translated *virtue* in Luke 6:19 and 8:46 is one that is often translated *power.*[9] In Acts 1:8, Jesus said we would receive *power* (same word) after that the Holy Ghost came upon us. The *virtue* that moved through Jesus into the world when He was touched is none other than the Holy Ghost, whom Jesus said would flow through our bellies as rivers of living water (John 7:38-39). You begin to see it, don't you? When we *fast and pray,* we open the *water valve.*

Next we consider how Jesus bound the strongman, and how we can break the power of devils over territory in our own lives by *prayer and fasting.*

Something to think about:

1. What did Jesus exhort His disciples to do in order to avoid being drawn into temptation?

2. Jesus said we must bind the strongman before we can spoil his house. Jesus "spoiled all principalities and powers" (Colossians 2:15). When did He bind the strongman?

3. Explain how Satan gains "place" in our lives. Use this insight to explain how Satan has taken hold in some areas of your personal life, in your home, your church, and in your nation.

4. Discuss with your spouse or friend the relationship of prayer and fasting to breaking the hold of devils. Think about how you might use prayer and fasting to break Satan's hold in your own life, or in the lives of your family and friends.

Chapter Nine

The Saviour's Fast (Part Four) — Breaking Satan's Power Through Prayer And Fasting

"Fasting possesses great power. If practiced with the right intention, it makes one a friend of God. The demons are aware of that."

– Quintus Tertullian (160-220 AD)

"I am not sure whether we have not lost a very great blessing in the Christian Church by giving up fasting…"

– Charles H. Spurgeon (Commenting on Matthew 17:21 "Howbeit this kind goeth not out but by prayer and fasting.")

The world is interested in the workings of the spiritual realm. Becky (my dear wife of 35 years) and I walked into a Walden's bookstore the other day. At the counter, under the glass case, tarot cards, and other witchcraft and pagan oriented literature and paraphernalia were prominently displayed. I asked the clerk whether Walden Books was a pagan bookstore. "You know, like Christians have Bible bookstores, is Walden's a pagan bookstore?" She was not flummoxed which flummoxed me. She jibed, to change the course toward which my comment led our conversation, and hurriedly led my wife to the section of the bookstore where we might find the item we sought. I jibed back! "Are you a witch?" She said, "No."

"Are you promoting pagan literature because of company policy?" I asked.

"No. The reason it's in the case is because of theft."

"Oh! Do you find that pagan literature is stolen more than other items?"

"Yes."

Pause, our eyes met, understanding my look and anticipating what I was about to say next, she retorted, "Bibles are also stolen. In fact, Bibles are stolen more often." She figured I was a Christian.

"Really!" I intoned incredulously. Then I asked, "Well, then, why don't you put the Bibles in your glass case at the checkout counter?"

Finally, she was flummoxed. To her rescue came her coworker with the explanation that her friend was merely pointing out that the Bible is the book thieves like best to steal. That is interesting! Thieves just love to steal those Bibles. Oh, as for why they displayed their occult literature prominently in the glass case at the counter, she explained that is what all Borders and Walden bookstores do. After a chorus or two of "we don't discriminate; we provide access to all literature," it was time for us to go on about our day.

I chose to regale you with the above anecdote for two

reasons. First, remember that when Jesus came, He entered into a world virtually possessed by Satan (Luke 4:6), where devils ravaged children in the streets of Israel's cities (Mark 9:20). Second, we know that when He returns, He returns to a world overrun by devils and the occult (Daniel 8:24-25; Revelation 9:20-21; 18:23). You have surely noticed the increased interest in the occult among our youth. If things continue along the present course, we will be exposed to the spectacle of children possessed with devils writhing in our streets, or on the floors of our shopping malls. Jesus began His assault on Satan's spiritual power base with a season of fasting and prayers. If we will effectively minister to our generation, we are going to need to learn how to engage these spiritual forces in spiritual warfare, and that is going to involve fasting and prayer.

Dominion belongs to God Almighty (Daniel 5:21). He gives it to whomsoever He will (Daniel 4:17-32). When Satan takes possession of territory (Revelation 2:13), he receives dominion over it by Divine decree (Luke 4:6).

Satan is given power (authority) over territory when those to whom God originally intended it yield their place to him (Ephesians 4:27). God gave the dominion of this world to man (Psalm 8:6; see Genesis 1:26-28). Satan seduces us to yield dominion to him by assailing us with temptations that appeal to fleshly lusts that war against the soul (I Peter 2:11).

When men succumb to fleshly lusts, they make themselves vulnerable to Satan's influence and control. This is not only true on the ground that by surrendering their will to serve these fleshly lusts they make themselves the servants of sin, and therefore, of the Devil himself (Romans 6:16-22). It also gives the accuser an opportunity to lay blame against them before God's throne which he uses as grounds for his petition to be given greater access to their lives (Revelation 12:10; Luke 22:31).

By the time of Jesus' first coming, Satan had succeeded at bringing the entire world under his power (Luke 4:6). Before Jesus could wrest the dominion out of his clutches, He had to bind this strongman. I believe that is what the temptation in the wilderness was all about. Jesus was beginning the work of binding the *strongman* in preparation to *spoil his house* (Matthew 12:29).

Jesus instructed us to fast and pray in order to bind the strong spirits that possess territory we must recover for God, such as that pitiful devil possessed lunatic child of Matthew 17:14-21.

O, brethren, the disciples had *power*; that is, they had the right to command these devils (Matthew 10:1). Yet, they lacked sufficient *potency* in their authority to effect deliverance for the child. Jesus explained the problem when He rebuked them, "*O faithless and perverse generation*" (emphasis added). He explained that the disciples' particular problem was a lack of faith (Matthew 17:20).

Perversity compromises faith, which is why we must add to it virtue (II Peter 1:5; see also James 1:5; 4:3).

Of course, the disciples were not *perverts* in the way we use that word today. Perversity speaks of any corruption of the flesh (Galatians 5:19-21) that soils our spirit, the filthiness of the flesh and spirit spoken of in II Corinthians 7:1. When our spirit walks after the flesh it becomes filthy with fleshly *perversity.* (Please, consider carefully what is next.)

The Holy Spirit dwells in the believer's heart and communes with his or her spirit there (Galatians 4:6; Romans 8:16). When our spirit traffics in fleshly lusts, it becomes filthy (II Corinthians 7:1). Our spirit brings this filthiness into our heart, defiling God's holy place. We sin to satisfy deceitful lusts; hence all sin is rooted in unbelief, and soils our spirit with fleshly perversity. When faithless perversity enters our heart, it condemns us; and the confidence of our faith is compromised (I John 3:20-21). In such a case, our spirit can neither commune with the Holy Spirit, nor come boldly before the throne of His grace (Hebrews 4:16).

Faithless perversity compromises the potency of our authority, because unbelief limits the "Holy One of Israel" (Psalm 78:41), and perversity grieves Him (Ephesians 4:30-31). Yet, He is the *power* of God given to us for ministry (Acts 1:8). (Are you following this?)

Fasting and prayer breaks the attraction of the lust of the flesh from our spirit. This frees our spirit to flee into the loving arms of our Father and receive cleansing through earnest and sincere confession of our sins (I John 1:9). When we have secured the cleansing, and confounded the accuser's claims over us by the blood of Christ Jesus (Revelation 12:11), the Holy Spirit surges through our lives (John 7:37-39) and begins pushing back the gates of Hell (Matthew 16:18), reclaiming territory usurped by Satan.

The crowds thronged Jesus. So, His disciples were surprised when He stopped, and demanded they tell Him who touched Him (Luke 8:45).

You know the story. A woman with an issue of blood many years worked her way through the crowd and sneaked a touch of the hem of His garment (Mark 5:25-34). He noticed because, as He explained, *virtue* had gone from Him (Luke 8:46).

The word that is translated *virtue* in Luke 8:46 is the same word translated *power* in Acts 1:8. We need to understand the relationship between *virtue* and *power*. To dominate some devils requires greater *virtue* than do others.

Here is the point. Jesus began His ministry by a season of fasting and prayers. I believe He did this on the principle that you must *bind the strongman* before you can *spoil his house*.

Jesus taught His disciples that to exercise their power in authority over some demons they would have to fast and pray. Since Jesus had rebuked them for being *faithless and perverse*, we must assume there is some relationship between faith and virtue and having potency in our authority. Further, since He instructed them that in the case of this sort of devil, they would have to pray and fast, we must assume there is a relationship between fasting and prayer and increasing faith and virtue.

We know that unbelief limits the Holy Ghost, and perversity grieves the Holy Ghost; therefore we can safely assume that *faithless perversity* interferes with the process of *virtue* passing through our lives into the lives of others. Furthermore, we may confidently assert that fasting and prayers serve to address this problem. Since we know fasting humbles our soul, we understand that by fasting we *humble ourselves under the mighty hand of God* so that when we *resist the Devil* he will flee from us (I Peter 5:5-9; James 4:7).

When fasting, I weaken the influence of the fleshly appetites over my spirit, and afflict my soul, so that my spirit begins grieving with the Holy Spirit's grieving over my sins. This produces deepening conviction for my sins and earnest and sincere confession before the Lord. The cleansing, available because of the blood of Christ, that cleanses us from all sin, restores me into full fellowship with the Lord. Then, the Holy Ghost can move through my belly like rivers of living water.

The *virtue* this world needs is the grace of God ministered to us by the Spirit of God. This virtue can pass through us and touch the lives of those around us.

O, that everyone who touches me will release a burst of *virtue* from my life into his own.

I am presently in a season of fasting and prayers. My mind is not so clear as I would like, but my heart is. I am fasting and praying about Intercessor Ministries and Brother Beckum's textbook on prayer. When I was called, and reminded that this article was due for publication, I began to pray that God would especially release *bursts of virtue* by His grace into the lives of all who read it.

Something to think about:

1. Does Satan have dominion over territory in your life? How did he gain this dominion?

2. What did Jesus teach us was necessary to bind certain powerful devils in order to break their power and cast them out? Can you identify some specific areas in your life where you are bound by sinful habits, negative thoughts of depression, anger, or fear? Or, do you find yourself consistently hindered by Satan from doing the will of God? These are strongholds of the Devil in your life. Make a list. Prayerfully consider which one to assault first, second, and so on. Plan a season of fasting and prayer for each one, one at a time, until you have assaulted all of these strongholds.

3. Is it possible to have *power* and yet be unable to wield that power with any *potency*? Explain. Does this help you understand why you sometimes find that even though you are a child of God, you have little or no spiritual influence when confronting temptations, or when attempting to advance the Kingdom of God against the kingdom of darkness?

4. Explain the problem of faithlessness and perversity and how fasting and prayer address this problem.

5. Remember the exhortation to add to your faith virtue (II Peter 1:5). Meditate on the relationship between *faith* and *virtue* and the impact this has on the *potency* of your *authority* as a believer.

Chapter Ten

The Saviour's Fast (Part Five) — Charging The Gates Of Hell, Bringing Down Strongholds

"The home church on her knees fasting and praying, is the great base of spiritual supplies, the sinews of war, and the pledge of victory in this dire and final conflict."

– E. M. Bounds

Many insights have enlightened us as we have studied the forty days and nights fast of Jesus, our Lord. Let us conclude our discussion of Jesus' forty days and nights fast by summarizing what is, for the purpose of these articles, the essential lesson we learn from it.

Remember, one of the enlightening insights we gained from our study of Jesus' vigil of fasting and prayer was that Satan had, by that time, ascended to such power that he could legitimately offer to Jesus all the kingdoms of the entire world. Satan gained this power by the same method he used in Eden. He manipulated man into disobeying God's law, bringing them into condemnation, and allowing Satan to gain the power of death over them (Hebrews 2:14). In this way, he established himself as *god of this world* (II Corinthians 4:4). God promised to send Christ to save man from the power of Satan. To prepare man for the promised Saviour, He gave His Law through Moses to serve as a schoolmaster, pointing all mankind to Christ (Galatians 3:24). Meanwhile, Satan used it to bring the kingdoms of this world under his power. Jesus is God manifest in the flesh, a sinless man, and the rightful heir of the Kingdom. However, in order to spoil the *strongman's house* the *strongman* had first to be bound (Matthew 12:29). Therefore, Jesus began His work with a forty-days fast, during which He overcame Satan's temptations and bound the strongman.

Jesus has left us an example that we are called to follow (I Peter 2:21). For, although Christ has indeed spoiled all principalities and powers (Colossians 2:15), and has received from the Father all power in Heaven and earth (Matthew 28:18), Satan continues to rule as "prince of the power of the air" (Ephesians 2:2), usurping Christ's authority in the earth. He accomplishes this through a network of seducing spirits (fallen angels) that teach doctrines of devils (I Timothy 4:1-4), bringing souls under bondage to his will (II Timothy 2:26), the spirit of antichrist that opposes Christ's legitimate rule in the earth (I John 4:3).

The God of Heaven calls us *soldiers* (II Timothy 2:3,4), engaged in a great war against the strongholds of a very powerful enemy, Satan, the "god of this world" (I Timothy 1:18; II Corinthians 10:4; II Corinthians 4:4; Acts 26:18). Our enemy is not flesh and blood. We grapple with spiritual *principalities*[10] that operate in the air (Ephesians 6:12), where the "prince of the power of the air" directs the "course of this world" (Ephesians 2:2) through those he may take captive at his will (II Timothy 2:26) by the "spirit that now worketh in the children of disobedience" (Ephesians 2:2), herding them to Hell while they are blinded by his lies (II Corinthians 4:3-4). God's *soldiers* are sent into the world to do battle against this enemy of both God and the souls of men "to open their eyes, and to turn them from darkness to light, and from the power of Satan unto God, that they may receive forgiveness of sins" (Acts 26:18).

The rules of engagement are unique, indeed; they are somewhat enigmatical. We fight an invisible foe, one we cannot touch with physical arms. Furthermore, we are strongest when we are weakest (II Corinthians 12:10), we surrender to attack (James 4:7), and we prevail only by dying (Romans 6:11). Stranger still, we do this dying daily (Luke 9:23; I Corinthians 15:31).

Our enemy, the Devil, constructs strongholds in this world, in our churches, and in the minds and hearts of men. Each *stronghold* is fortified by one of Hell's gates at which stands one or more of Satan's *strongmen,* devils guarding the gate to his assigned *stronghold.* From these strongholds, Satan exerts a controlling influence over territory in this world that rightfully belongs to Christ, to Whom has been given all power in Heaven and in earth (Matthew 28:18), to Whom be the dominion both *now* and *forever* (Jude 25; Colossians

1:16). We are charged with the mission to attack these gates, overcome the strongman, and spoil his house, recovering territory that belongs to Christ Jesus the Lord. We pull them down by the weapons of our arsenal, weapons that are not carnal, that is, not physical, but that are "mighty through God" (II Corinthians 10:4). Of course, these weapons include the Sword of the Spirit, which is the Word of God, and prayer in the Spirit (Ephesians 6:17-18). These work together!

In the armor of God, delineated in Ephesians 6:14-18, only one item is a weapon, the rest is defensive (Ephesians 6:10-18): loins girt about with truth, breastplate of righteousness, feet shod with the preparation of the gospel of peace, the shield of faith, and the helmet of salvation, are all defensive. The Sword of the Spirit, which is the Word of God, is the only weapon named — the preaching of the Word of God. However, notice what Paul, by the Spirit said next: "Praying always with all prayer and supplication in the Spirit, and watching thereunto with all perseverance and supplication for all saints; And for me, that utterance may be given unto me, that I may open my mouth boldly, to make known the mystery of the gospel" (Ephesians 6:18-19). The work of wielding the Sword of the Spirit is preaching, and praying supports preaching.

In fact, notice that Ephesians 6:17-20 is all one sentence and that the sense of this sentence is that we are to take our stand in spiritual warfare dressed in full armor, taking the Sword of the Spirit; and we are to do all of this by praying with all prayer and supplication. Prayer is the means by which we take to us the whole armor of God, including the sword.

When Paul sought prayer for himself, so that he would be given utterance, what did he mean? In I Corinthians 1:5, and II Corinthians 8:7, he observed that God had given the Corinthians *utterance,* which seems to speak of their boldness to preach the Word of God. Surely, Paul had this in mind when he asked the Christians at Ephesus to pray that he would be given *utterance.* In Colossians 4:3, Paul asks for prayer "that God would open unto us a door of utterance"; he was asking them to pray that he would have an "open door" (opportunity) to preach the Gospel.

Satan attempts to build strongholds that intimidate the believer from witnessing, strongholds from which Satan compromises the boldness of believers to preach the Gospel. These strongholds might be set up in our heart by fleshly lusts, the fear of man, pride, and laziness. Satan also erects strongholds in the hearts of those who oppose the Gospel and uses them to intimidate us, bully us, discourage us, and resist us. Furthermore, he erects strongholds in communities, where he succeeds at maneuvering authorities to oppose Gospel preaching. He might even succeed at establishing such a stronghold in a church. These strongholds must be pulled down!

We must assault the Devil's strongholds with the Sword of the Spirit, the Word of God. However, some are resistant, the strongman standing at their gate is too strong, and all our efforts seem futile. We pray, and attack, and pray some more, and attack with the Word of God, but still the stronghold stands.

When we go forth to assault one of Satan's strongholds, we must first *bind the strongman* that guards its hell-forged gate. We have a promise, "the gates of hell shall not prevail against" the Lord's Church (Matthew 16:18). Yet, we know that some *strongmen* are more resistant than others to our influence. When we come against a stronghold that resists our efforts, we must follow the instruction of our Lord, and use fasting and prayer to cast him out (Matthew 17:21). Only then can we pull his stronghold down and spoil his house.

Jesus came to spoil the Devil's house. He began by a vigil of fasting and prayers during which He bound the strongman. We are called to follow His example. I would like to relate to you a story illustrating what can happen when we do.

During the time I was pastoring in Ventura, California, the Lord impressed my heart with a desire to extend our bus ministry into a certain neighborhood of the community that was known as a haven for drugs and other evils. The area was cold and aloof, and not a single door would open to us. This went on for about one full year. I was amazed that we could not get even one family to allow their children to ride our bus to Sunday school. After awhile, I lost interest, and went on to other projects. A few more years passed before I began teaching the church about prayer and fasting.

We began a Sunday school campaign, and our junior girls Sunday school teacher came to me and asked if she could lead her class into that area to teach them how to knock doors and witness. She was relatively new to our church. I explained the trouble we had there in the past and was about to discourage her from following through with her plan when the Holy Spirit interrupted me and impressed me to encourage her to proceed, but to do so by prayer and fasting. She agreed. I called the church to pray and fast for God to open doors in that particular neighborhood, and many agreed to do so.

About two or three weeks later, this young lady began leading her class of junior girls into that same neighborhood knocking on doors, and, as you might have guessed, God began opening doors to us there. Later it became a fruitful field for our bus ministry and many souls were saved out of that area. The police began aggressively pursuing certain drug houses and key devil-possessed individuals moved away. The *strongman* guarding the *gate of Hell* protecting the *stronghold* Satan had established there was defeated when God's people got serious and committed themselves to prayer and fasting to bind that strongman.

Then, when we stormed the gates of Hell in the power of the Holy Ghost, they could not prevail against us, for greater is the Spirit that is in us than the spirit that is in the world (I John 4:4).

Something to think about:

1. What does God call us in II Timothy 2:3, 4? In your experience as a Christian, how many do you know who actually live as if they are soldiers in God's army? How many do you know who live more like they are on perpetual leave? How about you?

2. Discuss the "rules of engagement" mentioned in this chapter. Have you violated these rules of engagement? How will this change the way you conduct battle against the forces of evil in your life, your home, church, and community?

3. How do we dress for war and what are our weapons of warfare? Explain the role of prayer and fasting in our spiritual war against the Devil.

4. Has God called you to do a work, but each time you attempt to pursue it, it seems Satan gets the upper hand? Each time you decide you were mistaken about God's will, does it continue to nag at the back of your mind? Consider the very real possibility that Satan has established a stronghold of resistance to you, and it might be necessary to set aside a time for fasting and prayer to break the power of the enemy resisting the work God does intend to do through you.

Chapter Eleven

Fasting FAQS

Most books on fasting focus on its health benefits, including those written by Christians for Christians. As you have noticed, that is not the interest of this book. Our concern is with its spiritual effects. Although I offer a very brief summary on questions related to the physical and psychological effects of fasting, you should research this aspect of fasting before committing to a regular fasting routine and especially before you go into an extended fast (three or more days). There are many books that provide information about the physiological and psychological effects of fasting. You can research the subject by searching *health benefits of fasting* on the Internet. However, your best resource will be your family or personal physician. (Not all doctors are equally knowledgeable about fasting, and some are not supportive. Nevertheless, you should hear what your doctor has to say on the subject, especially if he or she expresses any concerns related to your particular health condition.)

On the next page, you'll find a list of the questions I will address and the page number where you will find my answer.

What should I expect to experience physically, mentally, and emotionally when I fast? (Page 89)

What should I expect to experience spiritually when I fast? (Page 92)

How long should I fast? (Page 93)

When should I fast? (Page 94)

Should I fast both solids and liquids? Is there any loss of the benefits of fasting if I fast only solids? (Page 95)

Of what should I be mindful when fasting in public? (Page 96)

Of what should I be mindful when fasting in private? (Page 97)

Of what should I be mindful when fasting for extended periods (three or more days)? (Page 98)

Should I fast routinely, and if so, how do I establish a routine of fasting? (Page 98)

What should I expect to experience physically, mentally, and emotionally when I fast?

The body receives from food the fuel it needs to function. Obviously, when we deprive the body of this necessary fuel, it has an impact on all of our bodily functions. Your experience will depend on factors like health, level and kind of activity while fasting, and your genetic makeup. Also, most of the effects discussed below are not noticed until you have fasted for two or three days, or more.

You will experience hunger. During the fast of a few meals, your stomach will become very noisy. If you use water while you fast, after a day or two, most experience runny stools. Most find that after two or three days of fasting, the hunger drive subsides significantly. Many describe this as their stomach going to sleep.

You will experience thirst. If you choose to fast both food and liquids, obviously, you will become thirsty. Dehydration is a serious concern when fasting liquids. For this reason, many choose to fast solids, but continue using water. If you choose to fast both food and water, pay special attention to your body's reaction to the fast, and be especially careful to have someone monitor you during your fast. Fasting both food and water (called an *absolute fast*) increases the intensity of all the reactions to fasting we will consider, both positive and negative. Please note, fasting water presents special concerns, and you should not fast both food and water without having someone monitor you during the fast. Having established the importance of using care when engaged in an *absolute fast,* some of the effects are as follows:

1. Dry lips, dry mouth, and, after a prolonged fast, slight swelling of the tongue. If you choose to enter into a prolonged fast, it is wise to use a lip balm.
2. Some testify to experiencing slight stomach nausea, and headache, but this usually goes away after one full day of fasting.
3. Remember that fasting both food and water intensifies all the other effects of fasting we'll discuss below.

You will experience physical weakness. The longer you fast, the more weakened you will become. A short fast of a meal or two, or even a day or two, usually does not cause one to become so weak they cannot function reasonably well. However, for some, even a few days of fasting can make them so weak they find it difficult to do routine things, such as dressing, or doing other light tasks. You will likely find yourself becoming sleepy. It should not alarm you if you can't keep awake. You'll likely doze in and out of sleep. Fill your heart with prayer and praise so that you slip off to sleep praying or praising and you'll likely wake praying or praising. The Lord can minister much healing to your soul during a fasting sleep. It's important to pay attention to your strength level as an indicator of how your body is responding to the fast, and this should guide your decisions about the level and types of activities you engage in during your fast.

You will experience mental slowness. Most people do not notice any significant loss of mental capacity after only a meal or two, or even a day or two of fasting. In fact, some report a heightened mental capacity. If you experience significant loss of mental capacity after fasting only one or two meals, you should mention this to your doctor. After two or three days, however, most people experience a noticeable slowing down of their mental capacity, and after a prolonged fast (beyond 3 days) some lose the ability to carry on a conversation beyond superficial queries that require little more than yes or no responses. On the other hand, some have such a constitution they can fast for several days before they come to this condition.

You will experience emotional instability. After missing only a meal or two, some people become overly sensitive, and unpleasantly irritable. Usually, once they fast a full day or two, and their stomach goes to sleep, the unpleasant moodiness dissipates, but they might become weepy. Some testify to a feeling of euphoria, an inexplicable sense of wellbeing and rest, while others testify to an inexplicable sense of foreboding and anxiety. Most testify that these emotional states alternate through the period of an extended fast.

Bear in mind that every individual is going to experience fasting differently. Also, your own experiences when fasting will not always be the same. The above, however, offers a relatively accurate idea of what you can expect when you fast.

What should I expect to experience spiritually when I fast?

This is a difficult question to answer. So much depends on what you do during your fast. This book is about fasting with the purpose of releasing your spirit from attachments to the appetites of the flesh to attend exclusively on God. If you commune with God in prayer during your fast, and meditate upon His Word, you will find that God will draw nigh to you; you will experience a heightened sense of His presence. As your spirit communes with His Spirit you will be given much insight from the Scriptures that occupy your thoughts. This is because of the primary and most desirable spiritual result of fasting, the humbling of the soul. For God is attracted to the humble (Isaiah 57:15). He resists the proud, but gives grace to the humble (James 4:6).

Warning! Fasting produces openness to spiritual influences. You must not accept every spiritual impression that comes to you. Not every spirit is to be trusted. "Try the spirits," to see if they are of God (1 John 4:1) is important counsel to remember. One way to steer clear of seducing spirits attempting to engage your spirit during a fast is to occupy your thoughts with

Scripture through meditation. When we speak of meditation here, we do not mean emptying the mind and making it vulnerable to the influence of any random spirit or notion planted in it by a seducing spirit. We mean to fix your mind upon the Scripture of Truth and fill your heart with thoughts that are inspired by them. It is important to test any notion you receive by the Word of God. This is true of notions that occur to you any time, including notions received during a time of intense spiritual experience in fasting.

How long should I fast?

This depends on what you are trying to achieve.

A routine, or spiritual maintenance fast usually only requires a meal, or two, or perhaps a day weekly, monthly, or as needed. A routine of fasting one meal a week, or one day a month, is usually sufficient to keep you spiritually sensitive, and alert.

A stronghold assault fast, however, usually requires more than a routine fast. When you come to recognize that Satan has succeeded at taking a measure of place in your life, and you are having difficulty regaining that place, you will have to engage in a personal stronghold assault fast. Indicators that you require a stronghold assault fast would be when you lose your appetite for prayer, Scripture reading, or church attendance. You might need a stronghold assault fast if some spiritually unhealthy habit has taken hold in your life and you have become awakened to the need to break free of it, but are having difficulty doing so. You might engage in a stronghold assault fast on any occasion where you intend to challenge Satan's claim to territory in your life, church, work, community or nation, and the duration of the fast will be determined by the strength of Satan's hold on that territory. No one can specify a specific number of days for such a fast, but usually it requires more than a meal or two and likely will require two to three days, possibly more.

You should not engage in an extended fast (beyond three days) unless you are convinced the Holy Ghost has led you to do so. Some indicators that the Spirit is calling you to fast are given under the next heading.

Essentially, you should attempt to be sensitive to the leading of the Spirit of God when you fast. There are times when circumstances will dictate that you need to stop fasting in order to take care of some responsibility. Of course, you don't want to lie to the Holy Ghost; He knows if we are sincere or if we are attempting to disingenuously excuse ourselves from a commitment to fast.

When should I fast?

You should fast when you recognize a need for it. Under *How Long Should I Fast,* above, we considered some of the occasions that compel us to fast. Add to that, the following:

We should fast and pray before making any major life changing decision, or beginning any major endeavor (Acts 13:1-3).

We should fast and pray when we are in deep mourning (II Samuel 12:15-23).

We should fast and pray when we need special assistance to understand the Scriptures (Daniel 10:3).

We should fast and pray in times of national distress, disgrace, or duress (Esther 4:16; I Kings 21:17).

We should fast and pray when the Holy Spirit moves us to do so (Luke 4:1-2). Let's elaborate, lest this seem vague. In addition to what has been mentioned above, when you experience a prolonged sense of urgency for yourself, some friend or family member, your pastor, some church member, some situation developing in your city, state, or nation, and you notice that this sense of urgency and concern either recurs very regularly, or maintains a constant pressure on your spirit, you should regard this as the Spirit calling you to fast and pray.

Should I fast both solids and liquids? Is there any loss of the benefits of fasting if I fast only solids?

This is a matter of personal choice. The purpose of fasting is to humble the soul and prepare the mind, heart and soul of the believer to engage God fully, without the distractions and detractions of fleshly appetites. It is possible this can be achieved with an absolute fast or a partial fast. As was already mentioned, however, fasting both solids and liquids intensifies the results of fasting. Usually, those who fast both solids and liquids testify that the results they desire are achieved much more quickly than when fasting solids only. As to whether there is any loss of the benefits of fasting if we fast solids only, the answer is no. It might take longer, and it might not be as intense, but the ultimate purpose of fasting can be achieved in either case.

Of what should I be mindful when fasting in public?

Jesus gave specific instructions in Matthew 6:16-18 for how we should present ourselves to the public when fasting. This shows that He intended that we would sometimes be in public while we are fasting. His instructions are all aimed at checking the spirit of hypocrisy: "Be not, as the hypocrites, of a sad countenance: for they disfigure their faces, that they may appear unto men to fast" (Matthew 6:16). He desires that we wash our faces and anoint our head in order that we will not "appear unto men to fast." With this in mind, if we intend to fast to the point it would be impossible to avoid *appearing unto men to fast* we should plan to conduct our fast in private.

You should use a breath mint in public when fasting, for our breath often becomes foul during a fast. The anointing of the head suggests the appropriateness of the moderate use of cologne or perfume also.

96

Finally, if you are of such a constitution that you can fast for a few days and continue to function reasonably well in public, be mindful that your mental acuity is likely impaired and you should not attempt to engage in conversation beyond necessary amenities. Be mindful of this when deciding whether or not you are fit to operate a vehicle, or other potentially life threatening equipment. Certainly, you should not attempt to engage in any serious business during a time of prolonged fasting.

Of what should I be mindful when fasting in private?

If you live alone, and you intend to engage in an extended fast, you should alert a close friend or relative and encourage them to call, text, or email you regularly during the fast. If you fail to respond within a specified time period, they should commit to come directly to your home and check in on how you are doing. If you live with family, obviously, your family needs to know that you are fasting and should be allowed to check on you during an extended fast.

Make sure your surroundings are conducive to the purpose of fasting. Put away TV, or any movies, videos, games, and so forth. Most find it helpful to fill the space with spiritual music. Have your Bible and a hymnal at hand. If you worship with an instrument, it is beneficial to have that instrument with you. Be careful not to become distracted from the essential purpose of the fast, which is to humble your soul.

Of what should I be mindful when fasting for extended periods (three or more days)?

Much of what has been said applies to this question. However, there are a few additional concerns to address when fasting for three or more days.

Sometimes your body will purge. This can be very unpleasant to you and your family. You might experience diarrhea, for example. A few experience nausea, and vomit. This is very rare, by the way, and probably indicates other health issues. Bring this to the attention of your doctor. However, it does sometimes occur and you should be prepared and prepare your loved ones for this possibility.

Finally, your spouse, and your children, or close friends, will likely become concerned when they see you weakened, and showing signs of dehydration, disorientation, and debilitation. Ultimately, you will be the one who will decide when to break your fast, but you should not arbitrarily disregard the counsel of those attending you.

Should I fast routinely, and if so, how do I establish a routine of fasting?

Routine fasting seems to be the pattern of the Early Church. Routine fasting is good for maintaining a desired spiritual alertness and readiness to respond when God's Spirit moves. It is recommended.

However, you should not become regimented in your fasting routine so that you become inflexible and cannot adjust to family needs or other unavoidable interruptions. For example, if it is your routine to fast every third Monday, but it happens that the Monday of your fast falls upon a day your family will be gathered for a special meal, it would probably be appropriate for you to skip that fast, or reschedule it, rather than require the entire family to rearrange their schedules around your fasting plans.

Establishing a fasting routine requires the same commitment and discipline that is needed to establish any routine, except that when it comes to fasting, certain considerations must be borne in mind.

You probably have someone who either depends on you to prepare meals, or expects you to enjoy the meals they prepare. You need to establish a routine that these people can accommodate reasonably.

Your routine needs to take into consideration the ebb and flow of your work life, or social life. Some find it very difficult to establish any sort of regimented routine for fasting because their workflow involves impromptu meals with clients, for example. Usually, however, there is a meal you can set aside for fasting that will not interfere with any of your responsibilities, and for those few who have schedules that make it very difficult, you should pick your opportunities as they present themselves.

Something to think about:

1. If you have not already done so, it's time to plan a fast. If you have never fasted, I suggest you set aside one meal, and during the time you would be eating, set yourself apart with your Bible, a hymnal, or book of spiritual songs, and pray and worship until you are satisfied you have entered into a frame of mind that you are in communion with God.

2. If you are experienced in fasting, but have not fasted for an exclusively spiritual purpose, or you have not fasted specifically to break the power of devils over strongholds in your life, then identify such a stronghold and plan to fast and pray that God would empower you to overcome the devils that hold that territory.

Chapter Twelve

Prayer And Fasting Diary

Prayer diaries were popular among believers in the early Colonial Period. Some of them have been passed down to us and provide wonderful insights into the prayer lives of our forebears. Also, they encourage us to pray. Not only are they a great way to pass on a prayer legacy to future generations, they serve to keep us accountable, and require us to examine our effectiveness. If you do not keep a prayer diary, you might like to use the following pages as a way to get started.

The diary pages are organized around the theme of this book, which is spiritual warfare against devils that require prayer and fasting to overcome.

When you enter into serious conflict with the powers of darkness over territory that has been given over to the Devil, you will experience very serious spiritual resistance from the seducing spirits Satan uses to hold that territory (I Timothy 4:1-4), and from the people they control (Ephesians 2:2). Satan is very wily, and you must be careful to wrestle against these powers in full armor (Ephesians 6:10-20). You will need to be on your guard.

Studies show that any action repeated consecutively twenty-seven (27) times in a meaningful way becomes a habit. By *meaningful*, I mean in a serious way with significance to you. I've provided a 6-day prayer diary. If you use it faithfully, it will help you get started toward becoming an effective prayer warrior.

Stronghold: Use this space to identify the stronghold you desire to assault. A *stronghold* is any place in your life, in your family, among your friends, in your church, city, state, or nation that Satan has taken and is holding in defiance of the authority of Christ Jesus the Lord.

Fasted: Use this space to indicate the duration and type of fast. By *type of fast,* I mean whether it was a full fast, or a partial fast. By full fast, I mean you abstained from all food and drink. By partial fast, I mean you abstained from some food, and some drink. For example, perhaps you continued to use water, but abstained from all else.

Journal: This space is used to record a journal of your prayers during the fast, and it might also include your prayers against this stronghold that continue beyond the period of the fast. I suggest you set apart a specific time of the day for your assault, and that you always fortify your mind with Scripture before and during your assault.

Date: Obviously, the date you prayed and fasted goes here.

Time: Sometimes you will desire to see what specific time it was that you were praying to tie that prayer to a specific result.

Scripture: Here you should record any significant Scriptures the Holy Ghost brought to your attention before and during your prayer time. Especially record any promises God spoke to your heart through His Word.

Insights/Impressions/Thoughts: Here record what insights occur to you, what significant impressions you receive, and any significant thoughts you desire to keep.

Report: Here you should record any activity you observe showing God's response to your prayer, and/or any significant developments or movements of the enemy.

Stronghold: _____

_____

Fasted: _____

Journal:

Date:_____ Time: _____

Scripture: _____

_____

Insights/Impressions/Thoughts: _____

_____

_____

_____

_____

_____

Report: _____

_____

_____

_____

_____

Stronghold: _____

_____

Fasted: _____

Journal:

Date:_____ Time: _____

Scripture: _____

_____

Insights/Impressions/Thoughts: _____

_____

_____

_____

_____

_____

Report: _____

_____

_____

_____

_____

Stronghold: _____

_____

Fasted: _____

Journal:

Date:_____ Time: _____

Scripture: _____

_____

Insights/Impressions/Thoughts: _____

_____

_____

_____

_____

_____

Report: _____

_____

_____

_____

_____

Stronghold: _____

_____

Fasted: _____

Journal:

Date: _____ Time: _____

Scripture: _____

_____

Insights/Impressions/Thoughts: _____

_____

_____

_____

_____

_____

Report: _____

_____

_____

_____

_____

Stronghold: _____

_____

Fasted: _____

Journal:

Date:_____ Time: _____

Scripture: _____

_____

Insights/Impressions/Thoughts: _____

_____

_____

_____

_____

_____

_____

Report: _____

_____

_____

_____

_____

Stronghold: _____

_____

Fasted: _____

Journal:

Date:_____ Time: _____

Scripture: _____

_____

Insights/Impressions/Thoughts: _____

_____

_____

_____

_____

_____

Report: _____

_____

_____

_____

– Epilogue –

Dear reader, thank you for joining me in serious, fervent, effectual prayer and fasting against the strongholds Satan has established in our land. To keep you encouraged, and to broaden your understanding of intercessory prayer and spiritual warfare, and to join with other likeminded warriors, I recommend you subscribe to *The Intercessor* magazine (2013 or 2014). The best contemporary book written on the subject of prayer is *Prayer For Revival,* by Dr. Benny Beckum, president and founder of Intercessor Ministries, Inc. I heartily recommend this book to you. To learn more about spiritual warfare, I recommend you read my book titled *God's War: Understanding Spiritual Warfare* (2013).

For availability and pricing, check the Intercessor Ministries website: http://www.theintercessor.org/, or my website: http://www.santamarialighthouse.org. Click on the Bookstore button.

– End –

End Notes:

1. Gingrich, Newt *Rediscovering God in America*, p. 21-22

2. Ibid. p. 22

3. Note: That Moses received the Spirit by measure is noted in Numbers 11:17. That Elijah received a measure of His Spirit is made plain in II Kings 2:9. Only Jesus received the Spirit *without measure.*

4. Note: There is some justification for the supposition that the *holy mount* of the Transfiguration occurred on *the mount of God* associated with the forty days and nights fasts of Moses and Elijah.

5. Irvin, Jill, *How long can a human live without water and food,* Staff, Food and Nutrition, Ohio State University, cited as source: Nutrition in Perspective, by Patricia Kreutler, 1980 (ONLINE) www.madsci.org/posts/archives/1999-09/937540022.Gb.r.html (1/14/08)

6. Note: I hope you caught the testimony this gives to the deity of Christ Jesus. Who was tempted in the wilderness, God, or Christ? Clearly, Jehovah God was tempted in the wilderness. According to the Spirit of God, through the Apostle Paul, when they tempted God, they were tempting Christ.

7. Note: We do not know the age of this father's son. We do know that he was possessed by the devil from the time that he was a child (Mark 9:21).

8. Note: In Luke 4:6 Satan acknowledged that what power he had over the kingdoms of men was "delivered" to him.

9. Note: The Greek word that is translated *virtue* in Luke 6:19 and 8:46 is δύναμις (*dunamis*—Strong No. 1411). This is the

same word that is translated *power* in Acts 1:8. It is usually assumed that this word primarily denotes authority. However, there is another word that is translated *power* that has this as its primary meaning: ἐξουσία (*exousia*—Strong No. 1849). For this reason, *exousia* is used in Matthew 28:18 where Jesus says, "All *power* is given unto me in heaven and in earth." When the word *dunamis* is used, it speaks particularly of the energy, one might say, the *dynamite,* that affects some work in the world. When Jesus did His works, His miracles, His wonders, it was an expression of His *dynamic,* which was the Holy Ghost. When Satan works his *wonders* (II Thessalonians 2:9), it is an expression of his *dynamic,* which is the unholy spirit. The idea of *virtue,* then, relates very specifically to the moving of the Spirit of God through our lives.

10. Note: Some confuse the *principalities* mentioned in Ephesians 6:12 with earthly magistrates. Titus 3:1, however, instructs us to subject ourselves to earthly *principalities*. The point of Ephesians 6:12 is that we do not wrestle with *flesh and blood* principalities, but with the *spiritual wickedness in high places* that operate through the children of disobedience (Ephesians 2:2). The antichrist spirit that operates in these children of disobedience rages against the Holy Spirit of Jesus Christ opposing His Kingdom authority in the earth (Psalm 2; Matthew 28:18-20; illustrated in Acts).